JIM LINEWEAVER, CFP®

Ohio's Financial Quarterback™

· YOUR ·
RETIREMENT
PLAYBOOK

OHIO'S GUIDE TO PLANNING
A SUCCESSFUL RETIREMENT

ADVISORS' ACADEMY
PRESS

T0089319

YOUR RETIREMENT PLAYBOOK
Ohio's Guide To Planning A Successful Retirement

Copyright © 2020 by James S. Lineweaver

Published by
ADVISORS' ACADEMY PRESS
Pompano Beach, Florida

FIRST EDITION
Edited by Holly Scudero
ISBN: 978-1-7341808-2-4

Book Design by Neuwirth & Associates
Jacket Design by Ray Mancini

Manufactured in the United States

10 9 8 7 6 5 4 3 2 1

DISCLOSURES

Lineweaver Financial Group and Lineweaver Wealth Advisors Headquarters are located at:

9035 Sweet Valley Drive
Valley View, OH 44125

They can be contacted at:

Phone: 216.520.1711
Email: Quarterback@Lineweaver.net
Web: Lineweaver.net

Advisory services offered through Lineweaver Wealth Advisors, LLC.

Certified Financial Planner Board of Standards Inc. owns the certification marks CFP®, CERTIFIED FINANCIAL PLANNER™, CFP® (with plaque design) and federally registered CFP® (with flame design) in the U.S., which it awards to individuals who successfully complete CFP Board's initial and ongoing certification requirements.

Information contained herein is not tax advice and should not be considered as such. Each individual's tax situation is unique and different. For advice related to your specific tax situation, please contact your personal tax professional.

CONTENTS

SECTION 1
PENSION TENSION

SECTION 2
GOVERNMENT EMPLOYEE
PLAN COMMONALITIES

SECTION 3
OHIO EMPLOYEE RETIREMENT
PLAN DIFFERENCES

SECTION 4
HOW TO PLAN FOR RETIREMENT

SECTION 5
THE CASE FOR A FINANCIAL QUARTERBACK

DEDICATION

This book is meant to be a thank-you to the caring and professional Ohio police, fire departments, teachers, and other city employees who keep our communities safe and our families well.

Our goal was simple: Provide you with valuable financial information in easy-to-understand language that you can use to improve the quality of life for you and your loved ones, now and throughout your retirement.

ACKNOWLEDGMENTS

A special thank-you goes out to my wonderful wife, Kathy, and our three children: Tori, Tyler, and Delaney, who keep me grounded and focused on what's most important in life. They are my inspiration and provide me with my drive and determination to always be the best that I can be.

To longtime friends Dave Scranton, who encouraged me to write this book, and Matt Crisci who is a prolific writer of 12 of his own books who helped me transition this book into something that we hope will be enjoyable for you to read.

To Geoff Powers, my marketing director, Charlene Niederhelman, my office manager, and Hugo Souza, one of my advisors who is my boots on the ground for the 36 cities that we handle the deferred compensation plans for throughout Northeast Ohio. They have helped me do some of the heavy lifting for the book and have worked painstakingly to make sure the book was up to date at the time of publishing and that we met all the compliance requirements for this type of publication.

To all of my wonderful teammates at Lineweaver Financial Group, Lineweaver Wealth Advisors, and LFG Tax Services, who are the backbone behind our organization and the real reason why Lineweaver Wealth Advisors has grown to become one of the Top 25 Registered Investment Advisors in 2020[*] according to *Crain's Cleveland Business*, and we have expanded to 26 states.

Finally, and not least importantly, I'd like to thank the hundreds of Ohio families who have put their faith and trust in the Lineweaver Financial Group for more than 27 years.

---

[*] Based on assets under management

INTRODUCTION

When it comes to the future, there are three types of people:
those who let it happen, those who make it happen,
and those who wonder what happened.[1]
—John Martin Richardson Jr.

R etirement is your future. So your goal should be to create a worry-free retirement for yourself and your family; a retirement that lets you live out all your hopes, dreams, and wishes, without reservation and without compromise.

Setting Goals To Win In Retirement

Winning in retirement takes some work; you need to remain alert to a constantly shifting playing field. Investments are no longer as secure as they once were; pension plans are rapidly evolving (and rarely in your favor), while accumulated assets require seamless coordination to minimize unnecessary taxes and maximize your retirement income. To put it simply, the best retirement plans require a smart offense and solid defense.

During the last 27 years, I've seen too many people lose their way, enticed by promises of silver bullets and the availability of mountains of free, do-it-yourself information. As most hardworking Midwesterners realize, *there is no such thing as a free lunch*! If you want to be comfortable in retirement, you need to be one of those people who make it happen.

While I wrote this book with Ohio state public employees and the Buckeye State's laws and regulations in mind, I also made sure to fill this book with practical, easy-to-understand advice that can help every family, everywhere, develop a retirement plan today, right now.

Professionals On Demand

Before we begin our journey into your retirement, I'd like to offer every reader one important piece of advice. Make sure all of the professionals involved with your money—CPAs, lawyers, investment professionals, and insurance agents—know your goals and where they fit into your overall plan. What I've found over the years is that most people have what I call "professionals on-demand." A lawyer they used once for a will; an accountant who does a great job completing your tax return but offers little, if any, strategic tax planning advice. You might even have an insurance agent whom you've consulted with from time to time for life insurance or annuities.

Having a Financial Quarterback can help create the opportunity for a winning retirement plan. When it comes to a Financial Quarterback, you have two options: Become your own Financial Quarterback to coordinate your financial affairs yourself, or else find an experienced Financial Quarterback you can trust to coordinate for you. Because you'll be making some important decisions that will affect your life for years to come, personal chemistry is important. To demonstrate the importance of financial coordination, I offer a few real-life examples.

Case #1: The Investment Withdrawal

Let's assume you decide to withdraw money from an investment, maybe as a gift for your children, to pay for a vacation, or to take advantage of a "hot" stock tip. Before you withdraw, you had better have the answers to these four questions, because a misstep can cost you *thousands* in lost assets.

1. Will you have to report the investment change as taxable income?
2. Will this withdrawal push you into a higher tax bracket?
3. Will the receipt of that income trigger taxation on your Social Security?
4. Will it increase your Medicare premiums?

Case #2: IRA Versus Mutual Fund

You decided to take some money out of your IRAs to help cover monthly living expenses, while reinvesting the dividends and capital gains from your non-IRA mutual funds to replace the withdrawals in your portfolio. Do you know the answer to these questions before making that decision?

1. Are you creating an unnecessary tax liability by taking money out of your IRAs instead of using the taxable distributions from your mutual funds to help pay the bills?
2. Have you quantified the difference in tax liabilities?

Case #3: Unimaginable Circumstances

One of my clients faced the unimaginable: her husband was diagnosed with terminal cancer. Under our stewardship, he agreed to make the tough decision to retire early.

Here's why:

1. We were able to trigger a 100 percent pension survivorship option for his wife, netting her a greater lifetime benefit, almost one million dollars more than she otherwise would

have received. If he had passed away before officially retiring, she would have only received the default option of 50 percent.

2. The client had signed for numerous student loans for his children. We recommended the loans stay in his name. After he passed, those student loans had a forgiveness clause and approximately $140,000 of debt was forgiven.

3. However, this forgiveness of debt can be a taxable event under certain circumstances, which could have caused an approximately $40,000 tax liability. By coordinating the client's professionals, his estate was structured so that the surviving spouse did not have to pay taxes on the forgiveness of that debt.

Each individual's circumstances are unique. Past performance is not an indication of future results.

Where To Start?

When I meet people planning for retirement for the first time, many ask, "Can I be my own Financial Quarterback?" My answer is always the same: "sure you can." Then I give them my pop quiz.

1. Are all the members of your team talking to each other?
2. Have you taken the time to research the many financial advisors out there and the myriad of financial products available to determine which ones are best for your particular situation?
3. Do you have the time to accurately monitor the stock markets?
4. Do you have access to proprietary models and research that can help you make decisions?
5. Are you staying current on tax law changes and how you can use them to your advantage?
6. Are all your legal documents up-to-date and written with the right clauses for your family dynamics?

7. Are you emotionally prepared to get kicked in the shins a few times? Younger people can weather these blows, but as you get older, you may not recover as quickly or as easily.
8. If you make a costly financial mistake, how long will it take you to bounce back? Will you be back in the game next week, or will you be struggling to recover long after you had planned to retire?

Thanks again for taking the time to read my book. I have tried to do everything possible to make it informative and entertaining. My goal is to give you advice you can use today as well as tomorrow.

Jim Lineweaver

Nothing provided herein constitutes tax advice. Individuals should seek the advice of their own tax advisor for specific information regarding tax consequences of investments.

SECTION 1

PENSION
TENSION

1

THE MATH
DOESN'T WORK

The U.S. stock markets have advanced considerably over the past decade. By most common measures, we have seen an overall increase of 200 to 250 percent since mid-2009 through 2019. The increase is well above the 7 to 8 percent annual increase expected based on historical averages.

However, most experts would agree that the probability of this strong uptrend continuing for another eight years or more is extremely low. They also agree that the stock market roller coaster will remain alive and well for the foreseeable future, even when the Dow Jones Industrial Average dropped over 5,000 points, or 11.8 percent, in two and a half months (between October 3, 2018, and December 17, 2018).[2] A little over 4,000 of those points were gained back by the end of February 2019, making for an unusually severe five months. Then, the advent of COVID-19 lead to record volatility in the first quarter of 2020.

With so much uncertainty in the world, some degree of volatility is expected to continue. It's reasonable to think that after the markets have gone through a strong investment growth period—that is to say, a long period of rising asset values—both public and private pensions would be on a firmer footing, but that's not necessarily the case. Individuals counting on their pensions certainly need to understand the inner workings of their plan. Will this plan be healthy enough on its own, able to cover any liabilities that come up and to provide the promised payout that individuals are relying on for their future?

That has always been the objective of a pension, whether public or private. However, in many cases, promised future payouts are underfunded. The plan's overall assets are decreasing while the number of retirees receiving payments is increasing and, thanks to medical science, those retirees are living longer than ever. This math clearly doesn't work, and it's the reason why so many pension funds are in deep trouble.

Bond Rating Agencies – Standard & Poor's And Fitch	
Investment Grade	
AAA	The best quality companies, reliable and stable
AA	Quality companies, a bit higher risk than AAA
A	Economic situation can affect finance
BBB	Medium-class companies, which are satisfactory at the moment
Non-Investment Grade	
BB	More prone to changes in the economy
B	Financial situation varies noticeably
CCC	Currently vulnerable and dependent on favorable economic conditions to meet its commitments
CC	Highly vulnerable, very speculative bonds
C	Highly vulnerable, perhaps in bankruptcy or in arrears but still continuing to pay out on obligations
D	Has defaulted on obligations and Fitch believes that it will generally default on most or all obligations
NR	Not publicly rated

Table A

Are Public Pensions In Trouble?

Moody's Investor Service[3] is an independent credit rating agency that, along with Standard & Poor's and Fitch, ranks and assigns default risk ratings to municipalities and corporations.

According to PEW research in their 2017 analysis, "The Pension funding gap of $1.28 trillion was only slightly lower than the reported $1.35 trillion from the previous year, making it the second reported decrease since the recession as the states total liabilities pass $4 trillion."[4]

The problem with many pension plans is that their contractual obligations and their liabilities are dreadfully underfunded. In order to meet their obligations and pension payouts down the road, additional money will have to come from someplace else. One auxiliary source could be pulling from the institution's revenue. This is the case in many city governments, where taxes are being used to cover the shortfall.

Another unfortunate method that pension providers are utilizing to fix their pension troubles is by reducing the benefits to those receiving pensions. In some cases, local governments have passed legislation to shore up their funding problems by issuing bonds; in others, they have even included increasing direct employee contributions as part of the solution.

But not all solutions include injections of cash from corporate profits (public sector), taxes, or current employee contributions. In 2014, the Multiemployer Pension Reform Act (MPRA)[5] was passed and allowed troubled pensions to reduce the benefits of current retirees if it was found to benefit the pension fund's overall financial health. Previously, it was unheard of to lower the amount of a retiree's pension, but this law changes that. Unfortunately for many groups of pensioners, parts of this law have already been implemented.

For example, a private pension fund serving the one iron workers' union[6] in Cleveland, Ohio, made history as the first to take advantage of this new legislation. The fund administrators evaluated all of their options, and even though the pension was still years away from insolvency, they opted to take drastic action. On February 1, 2017, the average pension benefit was cut by 20 percent. Some retirees had their monthly payment reduced by as much as 60 percent. For some, payouts were slashed by as much as $2,000 per month.

A *decrease* in income was obviously never the promise of any defined benefit plan, and as a result many former iron workers in the Cleveland area are now struggling to balance their household budgets.

A Vicious Cycle

For others, however, it's clear that it's better to receive less money after cutbacks than to receive nothing at all if the pension fund either runs out of money or "chokes" the company funding it.

In early 2017 at Sears and Kmart, retirees were made aware of how their situation may change in the future. Sears Holdings[7] has teetered on the brink of financial collapse for over a decade. Over the past 12 years, Sears has contributed nearly $4 billion to keep its pension plan solvent. Theirs is a legacy plan only and it does not cover current workers. The company listed its pension obligations at $5.2 billion, while the market value of the plan only totals $3.6 billion.

While Sears considers adding more funding for the plan, they are also considering whether they will be able to afford to fill store shelves; using capital to bolster the retirement plan takes from the ability to purchase inventory. And empty shelves may reduce future profits, which later will affect the ability to fund the pension liability shortfall.

It's a vicious cycle. On the one hand, an injection of cash into the pension fund allows the company to maintain the promised benefits, for at least a little while. However, if they affect future profits too drastically, the entire 125-year-old company could go under, and then nobody would get paid.

If you were an executive at Sears, what would you do? Or which would you prefer if you were a retiree collecting a Sears pension? Would you prefer a cutback in benefits, to keep the provider of the benefits healthier overall, or would you instead prefer the short-term cash injection, an injection that could ultimately put Sears out of business forever? These are tough questions that are being asked all across the country.

As you'll discover in Chapter 2, no one should expect Ohio's public employee pensions to ask their participants to vote on anything as drastic as the plan undertaken by the Cleveland Iron workers. It's my hope that the other public employee pension funds in Ohio and throughout the country will avoid this path entirely.

It's Time To Wake Up!

This is an issue that everyone relying on a pension needs to be aware of. Don't be a passive observer here!

In football, if the scoreboard shows you are ahead by only a slim margin and you haven't been able to gain any yardage, it's time for you to take a more strategic offensive approach. If you want to win, you can't just rely on the defense to do the work for you.

Fortunately, many of the strategies that the affluent use to stay ahead in the retirement game are available to everyone, even those in more modest households. Later in this section, we'll show you how to lay the groundwork for success by implementing these wealth management strategies.

One division of my company caters to actively managing 457 Deferred Compensation Plans[8] for public service employees and coordinating their pensions, insurances, and investments to get these clients ready for retirement. This idea grew from the personal knowledge I obtained by participating in many of these programs myself, and by working as a police officer to pay for my college education. However, the majority of my practice over the last 27 years has catered to executives, business owners, and the many affluent families throughout Ohio and 25 other states that rely on Lineweaver Financial to quarterback all their financial, taxation, legal, and insurance issues for a successful retirement.

I was prompted to write this book when I realized that many of the strategies utilized by the wealthy are not being taken advantage of by those who could benefit from them the most. In the coming pages, I'll demonstrate how you should use your options, and maybe even introduce you to some "big league" strategies you didn't know existed.

Pensions Are Evolving (And *Not* In Your Favor)

Back in 1875, when American Express[9] helped create the first employer pension plan in the U.S., the goal was simple—financial security and "peace of mind" for their workers. It was quite common in those days for an employee to accept a job in their late teens or early 20s and then spend the rest of their working years with that company. The pension was intended as a paternal act, a way that companies could foster loyalty, increase productivity, and attract quality lifelong employees.

This type of loyalty has been fading for decades. According to LinkedIn,[10] a popular business networking website, college graduates are now expected to change positions and even careers 2.85 times in the first 10 years after graduation. LinkedIn looked up similar statistics for college graduates from 1986 to 1990 and found they made just 1.6 job changes. The reason for this increase goes beyond the stereotype of restless grads looking to find their place and move up the ranks quickly; career changes are also driven by an increase in companies who treat employees as if their presence were temporary.

Pensions especially have undergone their own changes in the past three decades, in response to financial market turmoil. This turmoil has led to stock market crashes and low interest rates as well as an overall reduction in loyalty from both employees and employers. Huge price swings in certain investment markets have, at times, erased 40 percent or more of investor value; consequently, predetermined retirement benefits became risky for companies. Many employers have stopped offering defined benefit pensions, often replacing them with 401(k)s, 403(b)s,[11] and 457 plans. This gave employees more flexibility in the short term, but virtually eliminated any certainty of what they would actually receive when they stopped working. We'll talk more about these plans in the coming sections.

Are Government Pensions Safe?

Pensions promised to municipal and state employees are being put to the test in different ways. The risks to pensioners aren't much different, but the solutions being kicked around by city governments involve elected officials, taxpayers, and employees who have been counting on their retirement plan. The solutions also involve the many bondholders who have lent money to the municipality. This is one of the biggest issues affecting city governments across the country, but rather than look who to blame for the problem, it would surely be more useful to frame the problem and identify the various solutions being considered.

In Dallas, Texas, Mayor Mike Rawlings[12] declared that his city is "walking into the fan blades" of municipal bankruptcy. The big problem he refers to is a request by the managers of a pension fund of uniformed officers for $1.35 billion, in hopes of pushing disaster just a little further out into the future.

Dallas is not the only city trying to avoid the "fan blades." Rawlings's graphic observation is true of most city, county, and even state governments across the United States. At some point in the near future, they all must deal with the reality that the breeze they currently feel will eventually be followed by a sudden, severe storm unless they change their course. There is no longer a question of whether a new direction is needed; it's now a question of which restrictive or expensive recipe will feed everyone who needs it.

We believe going forward, the only certain outcome is that state and municipal employees will all feel the pinch. It may be in the form of lower pension payments, higher taxes, or working longer. For many, it will be a combination of all three. While waiting for the specifics of the inevitable to become clear, future retirees should take the initiative to solidify their own finances. We can no longer rely on the old team who used to watch out for employee finances. Workers should position themselves to win, no matter what happens. This takes a little repositioning, but it's absolutely critical.

Unfunded Public Pensions Are Everywhere

A report published by the Hoover Institution in May 2017 titled *Hidden Debt, Hidden Deficits: How Pension Promises Are Consuming State and Local Budgets*[13] found that unfunded liabilities of state and local pensions are still growing. The report determined the value of pension liabilities for 649 state and local pension funds across the country. When the analysts focused only on already-earned, guaranteed benefits, the accrued unfunded liabilities were $3.846 trillion. This number is 2.8 times larger than the values reflected in government disclosures.

The report also found that the vast majority of local governments are still relying on investment return assumptions of 7 to 8 percent. Actual investment earnings are usually closer to 2.5 percent. The Hoover Institution[14] demonstrated that in the aggregate, the situation is deteriorating as total government employer contributions to pensions were $111 billion, almost 5 percent of revenue; the actual amount necessary to keep the problem from worsening is $289 billion, or 12.7 percent of revenue. The prospect of investment returns moving back to historical norms or worse as pension liabilities grow will call for real solutions, not just financial Band-Aids or sleight of hand.

SUMMARY: Chapter 1

- Few, if any, pensions are currently on a firm footing. Plan assets are significantly lower than longer-term liabilities and are thus unsustainable under current conditions.
- The method of calculating estimated pension investment returns is flawed; actual returns are consistently much lower.
- Mismatch of investment returns versus pension outflows may be reconciled by reducing non-cash benefits.
- Many financial management strategies that are used by the affluent are available to more modest households.
- Municipal (and all state) employees may experience lower payments, higher taxes, or a longer working career.

2

HOW SOUND ARE THE PUBLIC EMPLOYEE PENSIONS IN OHIO?

O hio's five public pension funds hold a collective $210 billion in assets. These assets provide for the future of nearly two million participants in the State Teachers Retirement System (STRS), the State Employees Retirement System (SERS), the Police & Fire Pension Fund (OP&F), the Highway Patrol Retirement System (HPRS), and the Ohio Public Employees Retirement System (OPERS).[15]

Four of the five systems are also currently providing health insurance, albeit with some major changes that have recently taken place (which we will discuss in Section 3); note that none of them are legally required to provide healthcare. These pension funds are overseen by Ohio's State Assembly.[16] They have consistently provided on-time payments and fiscal security to those who have served the public and who now rely on them in retirement. As we're about to see, that system could be in great jeopardy.

•   •   •

The Evolution Of Ohio State Pensions

Soaring healthcare costs, including prescription drugs, have certainly challenged Ohio's public pension system. Recent dramatic turns in the economy, both local to Ohio and to the greater U.S., have also affected the pensions' outlook. Other challenges include the increased longevity of retirees and investment returns that are consistently lower than expected.

In the autumn of 2012, five bills related to public pensions came up for vote before the Ohio State Senate and House of Representatives. Each bill addressed one of the five public pension systems, making changes in how the pensions would be funded. Certainly, none of the bills were particularly popular among pensioners. Nevertheless, each bill passed the Senate unanimously, and only one "no" vote was recorded in the House. Senator Tom Niehaus[17] presided over the Senate at that time, and he expressed his resolve by saying, "We know the changes are not very popular, but they are necessary."

The bills were quickly signed into law by Governor John Kasich,[18] and their effect was felt just a few months later in January, as many Ohio public employees suddenly faced higher pension contribution rates and older retirement age requirements. Most legislators believed these changes to be a very good start, but many expressed their opinions that more work would be needed to shore up the funds that public employees rely on when they retire.

Overall, under the new laws, employee contribution rates gradually increased from 10 to 14 percent for STRS and from 10 percent to 12.25 percent for OP&F. The reason given by House Speaker William Batchelder[19] and others in the legislature for the higher contribution rate for STRS is that teachers live longer, so more money is needed to avoid a shortfall.

Unreasonable Expectations

These pensions were designed with a consistent underlying return of 8 percent in mind, and that's another problem that providers have faced.

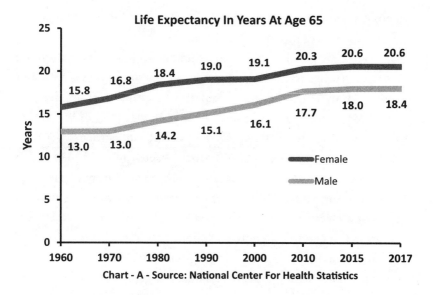

Chart - A - Source: National Center For Health Statistics

For more than a century, 8 percent was a reasonable average return rate to expect.

However, the current conversation among professional investors and mathematicians is not whether they should still use 8 percent, but instead how much *lower* than 8 percent would be more realistic. According to a story in *Bloomberg Businessweek*[20] published August 2, 2017, "The average target has fallen to 7.5 percent, but that's still probably high and difficult to meet without taking excessive risk."

The only reason pensions may come close to that 8 percent rate is because they are still benefiting from older investments, which carry a higher available yield based on the time when they were purchased. These higher yield holdings, which have not yet matured, are inching closer to that point. And low interest rates are expected to drag down pension fund returns for the foreseeable future.

This is a major part of the evolution of pensions up to this point. And it's a growing problem for the $29.1 trillion worth of U.S. pension[21] funds. Many of them are counting on getting at least a 7.5 percent investment return in order to cover promises made to current and future retirees. Declining investment returns are leading to a reduced pace of pension growth, and pensions will consequently continue to evolve to compensate. We can expect to see mandated reduced benefits and more infusions of taxpayer money in the coming years.

Why are these pension funds so reluctant to lower their assumed investment earnings rate even though aiming for such a rate is risky and imprudent? One reason is that calculations stemming from this rate include some political hot buttons. Effective July 1, 2017, Ohio STRS was forced to lower the planned Cost of Living Adjustments (COLA) when they lowered their expected return target from 7.75 percent to 7.45 percent. The next study to determine the expected investment experience affecting COLA won't happen for another five years. Prior to July 1, retirees were eligible for a 2 percent COLA[22] increase after five full years of receiving benefits. When you reduce or eliminate cost-of-living increases, even if your long-term intentions are good, you court voter dissatisfaction and are less likely to get reelected.

Longer Life Spans—Good And Bad

Another aspect that negatively impacts the reliability of U.S. pensions as a safety net is today's increased longevity. Actuaries may have correctly estimated the number of retirees that would eventually pull from the fund, but they underestimated how long people would live. Most of us agree that living a long, productive life is the goal and doing so can still create financial stress for retirees.

What was your life expectancy when you started working? As of 2018, Ohio ranked 42nd in the nation, with an average life expectancy of 77.1 years. In 1980, the average life expectancy was only 73.5 years. This means that, on average, every person who started working in 1980 will be receiving a pension from the system for four years longer than would have been expected. Those unexpected payments will really add up. This overall increase in longevity has a far-reaching impact on a pension fund's ability to meet its demands.

Ohio's Largest Public Pensions— Today And Tomorrow

The reforms of 2012 have reduced the urgency to improve the health of the system, but much more needs to be done for state pension plans to remain viable in the long run and capable of making good on their promises. Two professors of economics, Erick M. Elder[23] from the University of Arkansas and David Mitchell[24] from the University of Central Arkansas, did a study on Ohio's five public pension systems, which was released on December 31, 2016. The study is titled *Ohio Public Pension System— Traditional Funding Ratios Are Not Enough for Pension Funds.*[25] The authors utilized hard mathematical realities along with economic scenario analysis and determined that Ohio's pension plans are "falling significantly short on their obligations to hundreds of thousands of Ohioans." Furthermore, "Ohio ranks ahead of only Mississippi in terms of the level of unfunded liabilities relative to the size of the state's income."

How did Elder and Mitchell draw their conclusions? The report breaks down each of the five pension plans and how it applies both current funding and various rates of return on those assets, while balancing that against expected payouts and time horizons. The research is thorough and presented very well to readers.

The authors have even provided an online tool where a pensioner can choose their plan (OPERS, STRS, SERS, OP&F, or HPRS) and then pick their retirement year to receive a breakdown of their current situation. If you visit the website of the Mercatus Center[26] (www.mercatus. org/ohiopensions), you can access details on the study. You can even determine, according to their study and specifically for your situation, what the likelihood is of your pension failing to pay in full.

How Long Can Ohio Keep Doing What It's Doing?

As of December 2016, despite assets of $192 billion, it's estimated that the Ohio pension funds would require an additional $275 billion in order to be fully funded. With 11.6 million people currently living in Ohio, that cost comes to an additional $7,000 per resident. After running 100,000 scenarios and simulations, Elder and Mitchell[27] determined that Ohio pensions have sufficient assets to pay uninterrupted for the next five years. Their calculations suggest that it's highly unlikely these funds can maintain the funds necessary beyond five years.

Elder and Mitchell's research and analysis conclude that by the year 2037, OPERS—Ohio's largest employee retirement program—has only a 50 percent chance of fulfilling its promises. The situation is even more challenging for OP&F, which the authors calculate has less than a 25 percent chance of meeting its obligations.

The challenges and risks are very clear, and it's obvious that state pension systems need to take drastic action. With low investment returns, increased longevity, and a larger percentage of deserving pensioners beginning to withdraw from the funds every month, a more serious crisis may be forthcoming.

SUMMARY: Chapter 2

- Challenges to pensions go beyond the ability to make standard payments and include healthcare inflation and prescription drug costs.
- Most pensions were designed with the expectation of a return rate that is unreasonable in today's markets.
- Ohioans are now living an average of 77.8 years (versus 73.5 years in 1980).
- The study by Elder and Mitchell outlines the challenges facing Ohio's public pension programs.
- The system has become unsustainable. Either pension rates will have to be lowered or the system will need better public funding.

3

FUNDING VERSUS SOLVENCY

A pension fund's solvency is a measure of whether its assets are adequate to cover its liabilities. Pensions are funded incrementally, by employer contributions and at times by participant contributions. When the workforce is growing faster than the group of pensioners receiving retirement benefits, insolvency is less of a risk since the cash flow into the fund is higher than that being taken out. Of course, unending workforce growth in a finite world is only sustainable if income from investments can keep up with benefit payments. The benefits would include any healthcare expenses in addition to income payments.

Types Of Solvency

As mentioned previously, Ohio pensions are in a situation similar to that of many other programs. The combination of a lower income from investments, aging employees, and a large number of current pension recipients has caused these plans to become insolvent.

Analysts for rating agencies and others involved in monitoring fiscal health divide solvency measures into five groupings:

- **Cash solvency.** This estimates if a state has enough cash on hand to pay its current bills.
- **Budget solvency.** Does the entity pay its annual bills with revenue taken in during the year, or does it regularly face a budget shortfall that necessitates borrowing or using another means to balance?
- **Long-run solvency**. Each municipality has long-term financial commitments, and this type measures whether there will be enough money to withstand any unforeseen events. An example would be ongoing low or negative pension fund earnings when forecasted earnings are high.
- **Service-level solvency.** This measures if the state has the ability to increase spending if it is called for by either citizens or other events.
- **Fund solvency.** How mismatched are the funds available in a state or local government's pension fund versus its unfunded pension and healthcare liabilities?

Unaccountable And Unaffordable

The reality is that none of the measures above are supposed to ever stray too far from "solvent." All states require that pensions providing for state and municipal employees be fully funded at all times. Actuaries are expected to regularly review all the assets and cash flows of a pension portfolio and conduct scenario analysis using realistic earnings assumptions of the portfolio; in other words, business professionals are supposed to be monitoring pensions to ensure that they stay in balance.

These professionals compare any potential scenarios with liabilities and payouts the fund is expected to meet and then figure out the amount of contributions needed by the government entity (or government plus pensioner) to review if there are enough assets to meet those liabilities. If one were to combine the actuarial estimates of all state and local pensions within the U.S., the deficit would be estimated as high as $6.5 trillion.[28]

Economists,[29] meanwhile, are more realistic in their expectations for pension earnings, and some have calculated that the combined shortfall across the United States could be as high as $3 trillion. And in many state and local government plans, the gap is constantly widening because the governing body isn't making the necessary minimum contribution.

In different states, there are different levels of assurance that pension benefits will be paid. Ohio state employees in particular have a strong guarantee from the state, for at least the *promise* of payment. This promise does not, however, include providing healthcare in retirement; Ohio state employees may find this an unexpected challenge to their out-of-pocket costs. Retirees outside of Ohio, meanwhile, may find their entire retirement plan to be a false sense of security.

The federal government's fiscal stress is an additional complication for troubled pension plans. The trend out of Washington is to place more financial burdens on individual states as they wrestle with their own national budgetary shortfalls. This risk appears only to be growing, as the federal deficit is still rising each year. Each municipality is forced to develop their own answers to their multiplying questions of solvency.

For Ohio state employees, none of the solutions to this mismatch are popular. In January 2019, retired police officers and firefighters saw big reductions to the pensions that had been funding their health insurance. The explanation by OP&F fund director John J. Gallagher[30] is that: "This is all being done in an effort to preserve its solvency." These pension changes, and possible methods to manage them, will be discussed in a later chapter. The important thing to understand now is that fund directors and managers are taking big steps to retain future solvency. These steps have a huge impact on your future, and it's essential that you begin planning around them now.

•   •   •

Regional Rankings

On the whole, Ohio state retirement systems are 82 percent[31] funded. We could choose to look on the bright side and feel good that Ohio earned a grade of "D" from the nonprofit watchdog group Truth in Accounting[32] (TIA). TIA ranked 50 state government public service pension plans in 2019. Of those plans, 9 received an "F" from TIA. An "F" indicates a "taxpayer burden greater than $20,000." These plans could not possibly become solvent without a huge tax increase, which ironically would also come out of retirees' pockets as taxpayers.

Here's how Ohio and several neighboring states rank among all states in TIA's 2019 fiscal health rankings:

- Indiana—15th
- Ohio—25th
- West Virginia—30th
- Pennsylvania—39th
- Michigan—38th
- Kentucky—44th

Funding Pensions By Fixing Mismatches

Ohio's population ranks seventh in the U.S., but third when it comes to unfunded pension liabilities. In the short run, Ohio pensions should have no problems meeting liabilities. But when one compares presumed rates of investment return of 7.25 percent or higher with actual return rates that are much lower, the distant future becomes far less certain.

Over the past decade, the overall health of the plan has eroded as lower (and presumably more realistic) forecasted return rates are being taken into consideration. Some economists say the projected return rate should be as low as 3.2 percent, instead of the optimistic 7 to 8 percent used in most actuarial calculations.

This expected return versus actual return is just one reason a state may experience a funding mismatch. Mismatches can also occur when the cost of benefits increases faster than contributions to the funds. Ohio has discovered this to its detriment as healthcare, and later prescription drug plans, were added to pension benefits. The cost of these benefits escalated far more quickly than either forecasted or funded.

Mismatches have a long history of being met over time with a combination of discipline, changes in contribution levels, and investment returns somehow "finding" their average expected rate. The magnitude of the current problem may indicate that, this time, more serious measures need to be taken. Ohio state pension funds have already received additional funding from the state budget; they may also need to implement long-term strategies such as increasing employee contributions, lowering benefits, and scaling back future income for newer pensioners.

It's important to recognize the underlying cause of a plan mismatch. Is it the result of a normal dip in investment values? Is the funding not disciplined? Or perhaps there has been "benefits creep"?

Addressing the problem is easier for plans such as those in Ohio, where the combination of market and benefit creep accounts for more of the problem than does a lack of funding discipline. Despite this, public service workers who will be relying on their pension can anticipate that closing this mismatch will likely include a combination of larger contributions from paychecks now, low or no COLA increases after retirement, and increased personal expenditures for items like healthcare in the future.

New Strategies

Many people are currently wondering about the wisdom of relying solely on their pensions to fund their retirement years. These people are looking for new ideas and strategies to better plan for the future. Interestingly enough, these clients can benefit from the same strategies currently utilized by more affluent citizens.

The next two chapters will discuss why and when having strong defensive strategies is the right move regardless of your personal financial status. I'll also describe the positive steps you can take to move into an offensive position that will enable you to score more points and make up for any shortcomings you might otherwise experience down the road in your retirement.

SUMMARY: Chapter 3

- All states require that pensions for government employees remain solvent at all times. There are five different measures of solvency to be aware of.
- Many financial obligations have been passed from federal budgets to state budgets, which has added a further burden.
- As of 2019, Ohio's[33] fiscal health ranks 25th out of 50 states.
- Pensions need to take a more realistic approach to expected returns, and to plan around modern, lower interest rates.

4

THE BEST OFFENSE
IS A GREAT DEFENSE

F ootball and financial plans have an important commonality: a strong defense allows you to focus on the ultimate goal, winning the game.

Watch Your Back

In football, the stronger your defense, the fewer points your offense needs to score to win. When it comes to your money and your retirement goals, defense means putting a plan in place that will defend your financial position, your assets, against what we call "negative non-controllable." This includes things such as a volatile stock market, which can chip away at current rates of return; overall changes in pension plans that may reduce a city or state's long-term obligations *and* your monthly payouts exposure; and either increased taxes or reductions in available deductions (or both) that can affect your current and future wealth accumulation.

Don't Assume

When you took your position in public service, you may have handed the retirement ball off to your employer, knowingly or not. It isn't uncommon to depend on your employer to have your retirement years taken care of. You may not have spent much time thinking about your own role in securing your financial future.

At the beginning of your career, you probably assumed your income might not grow as high as that of others. But defensively, over the long haul, you believed you weren't going to lose. This perceived long-term financial security is one of the many reasons people go into public service.

I have personally known families that worked in the private sector who maintained high income during their working years but who are now spending their retirement concerned about meeting their living expenses. I know many more who have retired from public service, who had settled for a moderate income while employed but, in retirement, are now more carefree than most others their age. It's a great trade-off and a special part of your compensation.

No doubt anyone who has served the public for 20 years or more deserves the confidence to do a touchdown dance once they hit the working years' end zone. Sadly, like everything else in life, change is inevitable. It was a basketball coach named Mike Krzyzewski[34] who once advised, "Don't take special for granted."

Tipping The Game In Your Favor

You who have chosen to read this book, I applaud you for your foresight. You want to make sure you know exactly what's happening on the field. Let's start by discovering what setting up defensively means for everybody who is looking forward to enjoying retirement.

You've decided you don't want to give up any yards unnecessarily or commit obvious resource-draining penalties. Where do you start? The answer: know your stats. It will help to tip the game further in your favor, even when a win already seems assured.

There are a number of items you should start paying attention to now in order to accomplish this. Not unlike sports, you must study the opposing side—that is, the side that will financially work against you and understand that it will give you an edge. Just a few of the things you need to ask yourself:

- What are my expected costs?
- Using those estimated costs, what is my necessary income?
- How much will savings account for?
- Will my household receive Social Security? If so, how much will the Windfall Elimination or Governmental Offset reduce my benefits?
- Do I have any 403(b)s or 457 plans that I can roll into an IRA in order to take advantage of income opportunities and reduce hidden fees?
- If I do have a pension plan, should I opt for payment at the rate of one lifetime or two?
- How will taxes impact my retirement income?
- If I retire before I am eligible for Medicare at age 65, how will I cover my healthcare costs?

Family And Significant Others

Even if you feel your "off the top of your head" numbers are close, I suggest you sit down with your financial records and physically make a list of your answers to these questions. And then discuss those questions and answers with anyone else who may be affected by your retirement decisions.

Your spouse or partner may remember things you didn't necessarily think of, such as future plans for a new car or an aging relative who may have to move in with you. My experience has been you cannot assume you know what a "significant other" expects; you need to have a forthright conversation about it. Surprises in retirement can make it much more difficult, if not completely impossible, to adjust your game plan.

The overall goal here is to determine which decisions are best regarding your financial situation in retirement. Along with your pension, you need to consider other expected household income, your current asset allocations, and, if you're married, whether or not you will stagger your retirements.

For some people, entertainment and travel expenses might decline precipitously once you're done working. For others, those spending categories might become a greater portion of the monthly budget. This is just one reason why I suggest you have this conversation with all who will be involved. A joint conversation can quickly uncover if you've been assuming too much about your partner's plans and whether your retirement plans are far afield of each other.

Most retirees find their annual taxes are less than they were while working. This, of course, is not always the case. You're playing defense, so you should know ahead of time if this is your situation so that you can make plans with that in mind. Retirees also generally drive their cars less frequently and for shorter distances than those who are currently commuting to jobs every day. Car-related savings can include routine maintenance, gasoline, mileage depreciation, tolls, and more.

Hope For The Best, Plan For The Worst

You'll also want to determine if your true cost of living is going to decrease after you retire or if it's expected to increase. For most people, many costs go down in retirement. Healthcare coverage, on the other hand, is often a growing cost for people in retirement. We'll discuss some of the recent healthcare changes for Ohio state employees and how to help fund these likely increased costs.

When calculating costs and determining which will rise and which will fall, it's important to pad your numbers and err on the side of a few bad calls.

Remember, we're laying out defensive measures now, and by doing this, your overall calculations will be conservative, so you'll be less likely to find yourself coming up short further down the road. When I sit down with people who are preparing to retire, we make two side-by-side columns: one for costs they expect to remain the same and the other for costs they expect to change (either up or down). Within each column, there may be further gradations as well. Then we discuss and list all sources of income and savings. Once we forecast these expected costs, we calculate the expected income and compare the two. It's not uncommon at all for there to be a gap between expected income and expected costs.

Typical List Of Considerations

- **Housing expenses:** Will you be moving from your current residence?
- **Utilities:** Will your monthly bills increase or decrease?
- **Mortgage:** When will it be paid off? Do you have a variable rate that will increase?
- **Yardwork:** Will you be able to maintain your property, or do you expect to hire someone?
- **Home Repairs:** Any major repairs or upgrades planned for the future?
- **Property Taxes:** Do they increase every year?
- **Healthcare:** How much are you responsible for paying? When will you be eligible for Medicare?
- **Dependents:** Are you responsible for caring for children, siblings, or a spouse? What about pets?
- **Travel:** Where have you always wanted to visit?
- **Hobbies:** How do you spend your spare time, and what expenses are associated with those activities?

Keep in mind that this is only a guide, and there may be other things that impact some individuals. If there is a positive gap, more income than expenses, we have what's referred to as a windfall. Congratulations! You'll definitely still benefit from planning to use your assets wisely by utilizing the strategies in the coming chapters, even if the urgency is less.

But when that gap is negative, as is unfortunately the more common situation for modern workers, then we have a shortfall of income; it suggests a need to plan a method of utilizing accumulated savings. More often than not, there *are* ways to get around such a shortfall. This is where a Financial Quarterback who has a solid playbook and a trusted team can keep you from losing any ground. One key player, deciding who needs to get the ball while giving direction to other top professionals, can, in many cases, point you toward an opening you didn't know about.

How Much Is Enough?

A generation ago, the question was simple: "Do I have enough money to last throughout my retirement?" Today, with longer life expectancies and more lifestyle options, the question has become, "Do I have enough to live the lifestyle I *want* in retirement?" Not surprisingly, your considerations will also be different than those of your parents.

Where To Start

Simply put, the best starting place is to know how much you expect to have. Your pension plan statements should provide you with estimated monthly income amounts for various ages and a variety of scenarios. Know these numbers; I find there is no greater incentive for clients to accept overtime and other potential ways to increase future pension payouts than when they understand how it might affect their future.

Next, look at other sources of qualified retirement funds, including tax deferred savings accounts, Roth IRAs,[35] Traditional IRAs, 403(b) plans, 457 plans, and any annuities you might have acquired. It's sometimes wise to keep these savings in a tax deferred form for as long as possible and pull from these sources prudently because of how doing so will affect your taxes. These kinds of funds can be utilized if cash is needed for a major purchase or to fill an income gap.

If you don't have any deferred savings vehicles yet, now is the time; this can help save incremental income that adds up, or perhaps even save you from the heartache of loss. I have seen people in or nearing retirement lose 30 to 40 percent of their savings in a blink of an eye because of bad investments or a stroke of a pen that imposes a new regulation. This is a risk that does not suit most investors later in life. There are alternatives that don't expose you to these volatile swings. Playing defense can protect you from this agony.

Now add up the "paychecks" you'll be receiving. Note that many state employees are *not* part of the federal Social Security system or that you might be hit with the Windfall Elimination or Governmental Offset (described later in Chapter 10). If either you or your spouse has ever held a position where you paid into Social Security, you can consult your local Social Security Administration office for a precise estimate of what you can expect to be receiving in retirement, or you can view your statement online.

Add your pension income to your expected Social Security check. If you hold a deferred annuity that will begin to provide income in retirement, add that amount to your monthly income as well. If you own a rental property, add in rental income (minus any expenses) to your calculation. Lastly, add in any other possible sources of income you might have. Add all of these to get your final total.

Our purpose here is to get as close an approximation as possible of what you can expect so that we can maintain our defensive play; not doing anything now might be regretted later. Only when you have the facts can you determine the best plays for *you*. I've seen clients in a wide variety of life situations. I've seen some who would be better off if they worked another eight months. I even had one client who took a part-time job alongside his pension, and actually *increased* his overall income compared to what he had previously been making as a full-time worker.

Your analysis will allow *you* to estimate *your* monthly income needs, and help you determine if you should establish or increase the size of an emergency fund. This fund should be held in very liquid (easily accessible), low volatility vehicles—no stocks or equity-based mutual funds—and if you ever withdraw from it, it should be replenished when possible.

And this analysis isn't something you do once and then forget about it. I strongly recommend you review your anticipated needs annually, or whenever circumstances dramatically change, and take the time to create a new analysis as necessary.

Squeezing Every Last Dollar

We believe one of the most risk-free ways to enhance earnings growth and increase your retirement income is by minimizing your taxes. It's strongly recommended that you or your advisor determine if your investments are as tax-efficient as possible when it comes to taking required or any other distributions from your retirement savings.

My general rule of thumb is to switch the interest, dividends, and capital gains distributions in any taxable accounts to pay to cash from reinvesting. This will allow you to first spend what is already going to be taxable income, since you have to pay taxes on these each year whether you spend the money or reinvest. Doing this will also allow any other tax deferred accounts to continue to grow and compound interest until that money is needed.

Some people make the mistake of taking a fully taxable withdrawal from an IRA while, at the same time, reinvesting dividends and capital gains on other taxable accounts; doing this means paying a lot more in taxes than they need to. If, after taking this step, you still need more money, look next at your poorest performing tax deferred accounts.

The last source you should withdraw money from is a Roth IRA. The assets in these accounts were placed there *after* they were already taxed; they are completely tax deferred while growing and any income withdrawn at a later date comes out completely tax free! Keep in mind, though, that if this Roth becomes an asset that gets passed down to your children, they will have to take distributions each year over their lifetime, but those distributions will all be completely free of income tax. This can be one of the best ways to pass your money on to the next generation.

Hidden Retirement Income Bonuses

An often forgotten detail about savings in retirement is the actual monthly amount you're *currently* saving for retirement. When doing your analysis, don't forget that, once you retire, you will be able to stop making that monthly payment to your savings account, IRA, and other retirement funds.

For perspective, a woman once came into my office for suggestions after running the numbers on her own retirement income. She had calculated that the annual total of her pension and annuity income would be $12,000 less than she was currently earning. The number seemed shocking, but after a discussion about her current expenses, we realized that she was putting away $14,000 every year toward retirement. Obviously, those payments will stop once she's retired. When we ran the new numbers, we found that everything looked great. The woman laughed at herself when she realized that she was, in effect, getting a *raise* when she retired.

Another expense that can change dramatically is the amount spent on food. I've known couples who dine out frequently in retirement and spend far more than they used to while working; I've likewise come across those who ate lunch out most days during their working years and started eating at home more after retirement, saving a fortune.

Dining expenses is a good area to examine now, as cutting back can help you save extensively either before or after retiring. The most extreme case I found was a client named Mary, who decided to take up gardening after she retired. She thoroughly enjoyed her new hobby, and by eating her homegrown harvest, she literally saved several thousand dollars a year on food costs. I used to joke that she was growing her own money.

Another expense that often declines after you stop working is the cost of clothing. This is almost universally true of my clients who are teachers, as well as anyone who wears business attire. The cost of shoes alone can add up when you're on your feet all day, and the cost of dress clothes is nothing to sneeze at. On the flip side, my clients who are police officers and even some firemen often find their clothing expenses actually increasing, perhaps not surprisingly, as they no longer have a daily uniform to wear (and a clothing allowance to cover it).

Don't forget to also estimate the expenses you may spend on hobbies and other leisure activities. In retirement, you'll have a lot more time at your disposal to develop these interests. Considering the costs of different activities may also help you choose one over the other.

Pension Shortfalls — What To Do

So you've run your numbers, and no matter which way you crunch them, it's looking like your costs and incomes are not going to balance in your favor. What should you do next?

First, look at your side-by-side columns and the net figure to determine the precise annual shortfall. Add your non-pension retirement assets up. Do you have money spread throughout several 401k, 403b, or 457 plans? Consider rolling them all into one brokerage IRA. Doing this may eliminate one or more layers of fees, which I'm sure you'd prefer to save. That's one immediate saving measure you can make.

Next, crunch some more numbers and determine how much additional money you should have saved for retirement by the time you're ready to leave your job. Now take your shortfall amount from earlier and divide it into this savings amount to see what interest rate you'd need to earn to close the income gap. If the gap is too large for the current market interest rate, other adjustments will become necessary.

A big thing to remember: reaching for higher investment earnings at additional risk is *not* playing defense. Taking this kind of risk can actually make your situation much worse if the market doesn't perform in your favor. You may have to plan to make some other adjustments instead. This is why I always recommend taking the time to look at your retirement game plan five or even ten years before retiring. Safer, but longer-term, adjustments could include putting more into savings now, reducing planned expenditures, and considering working part-time in retirement.

Again, this is why it can be so beneficial to have a designated Financial Quarterback to talk things over with. Ideally, yours will have extensive experience working with the kinds of retirement plans you'll be covered under and who has a proven track record in making sure the rest of your financial team is up-to-date on the newest and best methods of maximizing your benefits.

Tips For Those Who Are Already Retired

If you have already retired, your options may be fewer. If that's you, the importance of a strong, *intentional* defense is paramount. You never want to give up more financial ground than necessary. The sooner you discover that changes need to be made, the sooner you can take corrective steps with your game plan to prevent an unexpected outcome.

If you instead find yourself pleasantly surprised that your income is exceeding your expenses, consider putting that excess away in case any surprises occur further down the road.

I find that many current retirees are not aware of strategies that could save them a bundle in taxes on their retirement funds, or even increase their overall income. Managing for tax consequences takes on added importance when a retiree begins to receive distributions from any tax deferred plan.

If you have the option between taking money from a tax deferred plan and another source, you may want to consider utilizing the other source first. Distributions out of a traditional IRA, 401(k,) 403(b), or 457 plan are taxable on the amount that was originally tax deferred, plus on any income accrued or accumulated on that amount. This includes Required Minimum Distributions (RMDs).[36] If you have other forms of savings that have already been taxed once as income, you should consider withdrawing from those sources first. There won't be a tax levy on each withdrawal as there would be from a tax deferred source. Given the choice, it's better to let the money in your tax deferred account continue to grow, with a beneficial compounding effect.

Once you reach age 72, you'll be required to withdraw a specified minimum amount out of your total deferred accounts every year. The reason these RMDs exist is because the government wants to be able to collect the tax earnings that you avoided when you initially put these savings in the account.

If you have a 401(k), 403(b), 457, Keogh, SEP, or traditional IRA, you'll be required to withdraw RMDs from your plan starting the year you turn 72 and in each year thereafter. If you wait to take your first withdrawal until April 1 of the year following the year in which you turn 72, you will have to take two distributions in that year, and then once each year thereafter. Therefore, *I personally advise retirees to take their first required withdrawal in the same year that they reach RMD age.* Why? If you wait, you end up being required to make two withdrawals in one calendar year. This increases your total amount of taxable income for that year, and may even cause you to move to a higher tax bracket. You definitely want to avoid that.

This is just one of many small defensive moves that can create tax savings. Over the course of your retirement years, these types of moves all add up. You can determine your annual RMD by consulting any good financial planning office or even the IRS directly; their website has very easy-to-understand tables, listing the amounts by age.

It is critical that you or your Financial Quarterback are on top of your situation here, as not taking the RMD correctly can cost you up to 50 percent of the amount left that you were supposed to take. The IRS has waited long enough for you to pay taxes on this money; they are not very forgiving if you don't take the RMDs and pay the required taxes on time once you're retired. Be defensive, be disciplined, and consider working with a professional you can trust.

RMDs are calculated starting with your age and are easy to figure out using the tables created for that purpose, although you'll have to do a little math. Simply determine the balance of your qualified plan as of the last day of the previous year and divide that amount by the factor from the IRS Publication 590-B.[37]

SUMMARY: Chapter 4

- Be aware of, but don't get frustrated by, money matters that are outside of your control.
- Get professional options rather than relying on friends and hearsay.
- Always try to improve your odds of success.
- Have you taken care of your family?
- Make sure you know how much you want in retirement for your particular situation.
- Take the time to create real numerical projections. Don't rely on guesswork.
- Leave no potential income source unturned.
- Get a coordinated plan in place, and review it at least annually.
- You can still work toward a better future even if you're already retired. Identify tips that can increase income or lower out-of-pocket expenses.

5

SMART OFFENSIVE STRATEGIES, NOW MANDATORY

S triving for financial success in retirement clearly requires a strong defensive position. As you approach retirement, maintaining or acquiring a solid ground to hedge against unrecoverable losses is critical. A strong defense is important; it simply won't be enough on its own for most wanting to establish a worry-free retirement.

Many people today, especially baby boomers, find themselves playing financial defense because of unplanned medical emergencies, rising college costs for their children, the impact of rising inflation, increased longevity, stock-market roller coasters, and what appear to be continually rising healthcare costs.

Healthcare In The Crosshairs

The Ohio Police and Firemen (OP&F) pension[38] system recently announced the elimination of all healthcare insurance for retirees after 2019.

In place of insurance, participants are paid a monthly stipend. This announcement is a *major* change. And perhaps it's just the beginning of other dramatic shifts in benefits offered under this and other public pension plans.

2020 OP&F Retiree Healthcare Plan Monthly Stipend Levels					
	Medicare Status Retiree - Spouse	Monthly Medical/RX Stipend	Monthly Medical Part B Reimbursement*	Total OP&F Monthly Support for Healthcare	
Retiree Only:	Medicare		$143	$107	$250
	Non-Medicare		$685	$0	$685
Retiree + Spouse:	Medicare	Medicare	$239	$107	$346
	Medicare	Non-Medicare	$525	$107	$632
	Non-Medicare	Medicare	$788	$0	$788
	Non-Medicare	Non-Medicare	$1,074	$0	$1,074
Retiree + Dependents:	Medicare		$203	$107	$310
	Non-Medicare		$865	$0	$865
Retiree + Spouse + Dependents:	Medicare	Either Medicare or	$525	$107	$632
	Non-Medicare	Non-Medicare	$1,074	$0	$1,074
Surviving Spouse:	Medicare		$143	$107	$250
	Non- Medicare		$685	$0	$685

Table B

Disappearing Fixed Pensions

If you're paid by the state or county as a public employee, you are among the very few workers left in the country with a defined benefit pension plan. In the early 1980s, the only retirement account for 60 percent of private sector workers was a defined benefit pension plan. Today, for those same private sector employees, only 4 percent rely solely on a defined pension plan, while about 14 percent rely on a combination of a defined benefit plan plus a defined contribution plan.

How has the pension playing field changed for public employees? Traditional pensions are still offered by about 84 percent of state and local governments. So why is there such a big difference? The simple answer—the political might of municipal employees. If an elected official were to directly target public employee pensions, that official would most likely not be reelected. As beneficial as this may be to you, the ultimate outcome has been that a large number of public-sector pension plans fall short of having enough money in their pool to cover expected payouts, as those in charge fear taking measures to keep them solvent.

The Bottom Line

The bottom line here is that most pension plans have been diminishing their benefits over time; this is the new normal. There's also no question that other modifications of older pension benefits will be forthcoming. And planning around any future changes is, of course, impossible without knowing what they'll be.

So it's not surprising that the financial stance that many have taken up includes defense against unforeseen hardships and being more proactive overall.

As I often remind my clients, these inevitable changes (and others we cannot even contemplate) aren't the end of the world once you accept this new normal. The key is to build a solid offensive playbook filled with strategies that place more of the emphasis on winning, without regard to what goes on at the pension end of the playing field.

Take your offensive game up several notches by deciding that you'll grab control of your success, rather than leaving things outside your control and hoping to have a victory handed to you. This "attack" is smarter, safer, and ever-more necessary. Like it or not, you're in the middle of the field now; you need to protect against losses, but you also need to play to win.

You will not advance down the retirement field financially by standing still. If you choose not to be the one to change, your retirement game will become increasingly more difficult to win. Doing nothing could mean higher taxes, lower lifetime payouts, and significant lifestyle shortfalls. Choosing offensive plays that help you win means thinking differently overall. Your employer has provided you with a starter plan;

it's up to you to utilize your ability to enhance it. And if you are willing to keep abreast of developments and do the proper research, you can invent and call your own offensive plays.

For those of you who might not be that adventurous or wish to spend your free time on other things, it might be reassuring to know, for the past 27 years, the Lineweaver Group of Companies has been focused on the needs of public service employees in the Buckeye State. It's worth noting that the guidance we offer in this book borrows heavily from the strategies we have implemented successfully for many of our clients and their families.

Learn From The Affluent

Perhaps you've heard the term "family office." These became more popular among the super-affluent at the beginning of the new millennium. A family office provides private wealth management for ultra-high-net-worth families and investors. These offices distinguish themselves from other wealth or investment management firms by providing teams of professionals that are all connected and working together. These professionals know their clients' business, and they are affiliated with other professionals who help in the running of the families' assets as a business would.

If you think about it, this kind of organization makes so much sense and is a powerful setup for the family. There are many nuances involved in managing any amount of money, big or small. And unfortunately, most of us don't have at our fingertips a team that includes an investment analyst, a lawyer, a tax strategist, an insurance expert, and a health-care expert.

To manage their family wealth more effectively, the truly affluent may have a team of these professionals and more who work in conjunction with one another to provide coordinated investment management. These professionals work as a team, so their individual recommendations can be woven together into one plan to promote that family's tax minimization strategy. If the assets owned by the family need estate planning or if other legal issues crop up, the team members who are experts in those particular fields work with the others to create a comprehensive strategy that maximizes benefit, minimizes costs (such as fees or taxes), and provides any desired and necessary legal protections.

The concept of a money management team makes sense and allows for just about every aspect of a family's financial life to come together. Even the savviest family will come across areas where no one individual financial guru has the necessary expertise, whereas a team helps to ensure that there's always the right professional for the job. With a team, each member can spend their time doing what they do best, and let a different expert handle the rest.

That's what the Lineweaver Process is all about. First, clients are assigned a Financial Quarterback to help coordinate their investment and retirement needs. The Quarterback then draws upon the expertise of the Lineweaver Wealth Watch Center to build, monitor, and update the plan with the help of our experienced in-house staff and coordinated team of professionals that includes tax, legal, estate planning, insurance, and investment experts to save clients time, money, and worry. It's like having your own family practice working for you, without the costs of a family practice.

By way of example, what follows are six interesting offensive strategies that our clients use in full or in part.

Real Estate As A Wealth Generator

When it comes to investing, we've been conditioned to think about stocks, mutual funds, and perhaps even certificates of deposit (CDs) as the best (or the only) options. And we tend to think of real estate primarily as something we buy to live in. But as far as asset classes are concerned, real estate property has been a powerful wealth generator even before the U.S. had a stock market.

We are all surrounded by real estate, and many people understand the market valuations and the cost of investment better than that of most other investment assets. So why isn't real estate more popular?

One of the reasons real estate is ignored as an asset class is because ownership can sometimes be time-consuming, both in terms of acquiring it in the first place as well as in its maintenance and upkeep.

Another theory is that because the real estate market is fragmented, there is no way to overtly advertise the benefits of ownership in the way stock brokers and mutual funds can use major media outlets for marketing. We simply don't *hear* about real estate ownership regularly as an asset class.

Investing in real estate means any method of seeking to earn money by owning or operating real property. At the most basic level, one can purchase land and hope that the value appreciates over time, while only paying taxes and any other related maintenance. A little more complex is purchasing and speculating on an existing house or building, making improvements, and hoping to later resell it at a price above the total cost of purchase and improvements.

The more popular way that middle- or upper-income people invest in real estate is through owning rental property. The primary goal is to provide an income stream—ideally, the amount being taken in from renters is greater than the amount being spent on mortgage costs, taxes, and maintenance. A secondary goal is appreciation of overall property value.

Many of us have friends or relatives who have amassed a high net worth from rentals; many of us have also had, or know people who have had, nightmare tenants. This is one of the major risks in real estate. Another risk is that property values have not had a smooth upward increase in prices over the past thirty years. Overspeculation in real estate, just as in other markets, can create a bubble, which leads to price correction, or bubble bursting, before prices can start to head back up.

One attraction of owning rental real estate is that you might be able to get a tax break on the rental's income through depreciation. Depending on your household income level, certain deductions are allowed to shelter the real estate profits coming in after you have paid for maintenance, insurance, mortgage interest, and taxes.

Holdings in real estate don't have to be residential, either. Commercial real estate may also consist of office buildings, strip malls, storage units, hotels, and more. As with the stock market, each real estate sector has its own nuances and concerns. For example, office buildings have longer-term leases than storage units. During periods of rising rental rates, the storage unit rental rates will change quicker than those of commercial rental. These fluctuating rates affect the underlying value of the property.

A large part of the power of investing in real estate lies in leverage. This power can work against you in the same way it works for you, though, especially if your goal is appreciation or improving the property. Let's discuss the underlying consideration of this asset class.

Let's say a 45-year-old school administrator has decided to put $40,000 toward the cost of his first rental property. He finds a nearby townhouse offered at $212,000 and negotiates the price down to $200,000. Our investor puts 20 percent down and borrows $160,000 to cover the rest. He now has the risk and reward on price movements of a $200,000 asset, but only paid $40,000 out of pocket.

The overall upward trends in real estate prices have often helped people to gain wealth, because they are earning something much larger than their out-of-pocket cost. What the investor in our above story needs to consider is that a 10 percent drop in his real estate holding ($20,000) is actually a 50 percent drop in his initial equity stake (the down payment of $40,000). I like to point this out because although, over time, leverage has worked in favor of investors, there are people who would never buy a stock with borrowed money yet don't think twice about investing in real estate this way.

The flipside is that a 10 percent increase in the property value equates to a 50 percent rate of return. These types of price swings are not usually the motivation for buying real estate, however, unless you are trying to flip the house for a quick profit. Most people like real estate because it provides a steady income; this amounts essentially to having someone else help pay off the debt, which comes with the additional hope that the assets appreciate in value over time.

Each individual's situation is different, and like all investments, real estate investing requires risk. Real estate investing may not be appropriate for everyone.

Transferring Real Estate To Defer Capital Gains

One of the great advantages of real estate is a little-known section of the tax code called a 1031[39] exchange, which allows an investor to sell a property and then reinvest any proceeds into a new property, deferring any capital gains taxes in the process (it means not paying them in the current tax year).

Originally, 1031 cases were intended to be simultaneous transfers of ownership, but in 1979 the Ninth Circuit Court of Appeals ruled in a case called *Starker v. the United States* that a contract to exchange properties in the future is essentially the same thing as simultaneous transfer. This case led to the establishment of the Starker Exchange.[40]

It is under this case that real property sellers with a capital gain may elect to use those profits to purchase a new property. To utilize this deferment, the taxpayer must determine which property being sold will be part of the exchange *before* closing, identify a replacement property within 45 days of that closing date, and then *acquire* that replacement property within 180 days of closing.

This ruling is a great way for small investors to gradually acquire larger pieces of property; one can start with a small rental, such as a single-family home, exchange it for a double or a duplex, and then later exchange it again for a six- or eight-unit apartment building, with taxes being deferred all along the way due to what's legally considered a transfer. Of course, when you stop transferring the properties and ultimately sell the apartment building outright, taxes *will* be owed.

Imagine how fast your money can build when you put off having to pay taxes in this way, trading up to larger and larger properties that keep paying you more monthly cash flow. This is why you often hear of very wealthy families that own a lot of real estate. They can keep growing their empire without having to pay any capital gains taxes along the way.

Family Limited Partnerships

A skeptic may ask, "Why bother to defer taxes on real estate when Uncle Sam will have to be paid at a later date anyway?" The simple answer is that perhaps you'll never sell the property; perhaps you'll choose instead to pass it on to your children or another relative.

There are some advanced financial planning techniques that can also aid in the transfer of businesses and property to the next generation. One of them is a Family Limited Partnership (FLP).[41] FLPs are frequently used to move wealth from one generation to the next; they can be a useful structure for holding and transferring real estate within a family.

FLPs are typically holding companies, acting as an entity that holds the property contributed to by the members. FLPs have several benefits. They allow family members with aligned interests to pool resources, thus lowering legal, accounting, and investing costs. They allow one family member, typically the General Partner (GP), to move assets to other family members (often children who are Limited Partners,[42] or LPs), while still retaining control over the assets. Because the LPs have no rights of control, they cannot liquidate their partnership interests. The timing and amounts of distributions are the sole exclusive prerogative of the GP. That is, a distribution cannot be made to one partner (GP or LP) unless all partners receive their pro rata portion of any distributions.

Because of this, assets are usually transferred at a discount—an outsider often doesn't want to own shares in a company with so many family members involved. When used for the right reasons, an FLP can be a great way to transfer and protect assets for the next generation.

Passive Real Estate Investments

If you like the idea of real estate but don't want a call at 2:00 a.m. when the hot water tank goes, there are other, more passive ways to own real estate.

One way is by purchasing individual stocks, mutual funds, or Exchange Traded Funds (ETF)[43] that invest in real estate and trade on the open market. One of the nice things about buying real estate invest-ments like this is that you can let the professional managers have all the headaches while you diversify into many sectors like hotels, apartment buildings, storage facilities, healthcare, big box, commercial, and more, and you can liquidate them fairly quickly as needed. However, you will still have to deal with market fluctuations and, like most investments, your principal will not be protected.

These types of investments usually do have attractive yields, but you have to do your homework or work with a professional who knows the field. It's important to narrow down the selection process and perform some due diligence before you put your money at risk.

Strategic Use Of Credit

It's clear that borrowing money can actually have a very positive impact on your wealth accumulation if it's invested thoughtfully. But how do you decide when it's smart to borrow? When deciding to use credit in *any* area of your life, a simple rule of thumb is to ask yourself, "Is this a smart investment?" The answer may be different for each individual, even for the same purchase.

For example, if I were to take out a student loan to go to college for a degree in ancient Greek culture in order to satisfy a personal interest in the subject, that would *not* be a sound investment. There may be a payoff in the form of greater knowledge and personal satisfaction, but there is no financial reward to offset the financial cost. If, on the other hand, I borrowed money to send my daughter to college to study dentistry, I'd be more comfortable with that debt due to a greater chance of financial reward. This is why revolving debt for average consumer purchases rarely makes sense; borrowed money should meet the investment test.

The same is true of major purchases such as a car for individual use. The nature of depreciation typically would make that a luxury, not an investment. If, however, a car or truck is required to maintain a business or a job, then borrowing to own it now (rather than saving the money to purchase it outright at a later date) will earn you more money over time and qualify that purchase as an investment. You may well want to use credit to purchase it.

The affluent don't maintain high revolving credit card debt, but many are fearless with thoughtful borrowing in order to build an empire.

Net Unrealized Appreciation

If you or your spouse works for a publicly traded company, don't ignore this rule! The Net Unrealized Appreciation (NUA)[44] is the difference in value between the average cost basis and the current market value of stock shares held in an employer tax deferred account, such as a 401(k). This only applies if the stock of the company for which you are (or were) an employee has appreciated in value.

Most distributions from a 401(k) are taxed at your ordinary income tax rate, which can be substantially higher than the current capital gains rates. To take advantage of NUA, you'll need to roll 100 percent of your employer stock out of the retirement plan all at once, pay personal income tax on the average cost of the shares at that time, and then not sell any shares for 12 months after the transfer.

Net Unrealized Appreciation (NUA) In Action		
Total Value Of Employer Stock	Stock Is Rolled Over To An IRA	NUA – Stock Is Transferred To A Taxable Account
Cost Basis Of $200,000	$1,000,000	
NUA Of $800,000		
Income Tax At Distribution	Rollover Is Tax Free	$70,000 (35% On $200,000)
Tax When Stock Is Distributed At Market Value ($1,000,000)	$350,000 (35% On $1,000,000)	$120,000 (15% Capital Gain On $800,000 NUA)
Total Tax Paid	$350,000	$190,000
Tax Savings	$0	$160,000

Table C

The remaining gains in the shares over the cost basis will remain deferred for 12 months, after which time you can then sell any or all of the shares and pay the lower long-term capital gains tax rates on the appreciation.

There are many hoops you need to jump through in order to get these shares to the lower capital gains rates, but the tax savings can be well worth it. Make sure you're working with someone who is familiar with NUA, so it gets done correctly. We also recommend you consult your tax advisor to make sure this strategy is right for you.

If You're 72
And Have To Take Out Distributions

With the Tax Cut and Jobs Act of 2017,[45] many retired Americans saw big changes in 2018. One particularly important change is that the standard tax deduction has doubled; consequently, many people won't be able to deduct their charitable contributions from their annual taxes.

Therefore, if you're age 70 1/2 or older, you might want to consider a Qualified Charitable Distribution[46] (QCD). The QCD allows people aged 70 1/2 and older to transfer up to $100,000 from their retirement accounts to a charity of their choice without paying any taxes. At age 72, taxpayers must begin withdrawing an RMD; the QCD can fulfill that obligation. Keep in mind, QCDs may be reduced by any IRA contributions.

The QCD also has the added benefit of keeping some taxpayers' incomes low enough to possibly avoid paying Medicare premiums (the additional fees that higher-income consumers must pay for Medicare coverage). By using this strategy, your charity still receives their money, but you avoid paying any taxes on your contribution, and you keep all of your standard deductions, too.

SUMMARY: Chapter 5

- Pensions are changing. Diminishing benefits have become the new "normal."
- Choose offense and decide you'll play to win regardless of conditions. Build a team that will work *together* to help you win.
- Real estate is a powerful and often underutilized wealth generator. Use of the Starker Exchange can allow you to defer capital gains.
- Help hedge assets for future generations by forming a limited family partnership.
- If appropriate, don't be afraid to borrow money if doing so will help you accumulate more wealth.
- Net Unrealized Appreciation: Wait a little longer and pay less in capital gains.
- Qualified charitable distributions may help offset your regular RMDs.

SECTION 2

GOVERNMENT EMPLOYEE PLAN COMMONALITIES

6

DEFERRED COMPENSATION: 403(B) & 457(B) PLANS

With all the pension changes we talked about in the previous chapters, one of the best ways to get back on the offensive is to be proactive and take advantage of the defined contribution plans you have at work. This will most likely be a 403(b) or 457(b) for state and local governments.

403(b) Plans

When thinking of retirement plans, the first one that likely comes to mind is the 401(k), offered by many private sector jobs. Employees of public schools and certain other tax exempt organizations, however, offer 403(b) plans. Similar to the 401(k), a 403(b) plan is a tax-sheltered investment, until you begin to take distributions. The underlying assets in a 403(b) can take the form of an annuity contract or an investment fund-based platform.

There are three primary benefits to taking advantage of a 403(b) plan.[47]

First: The money that goes into the account is pre-tax, so it comes from your paycheck without the IRS first withholding federal and state taxes; social security will still be withheld, however.

Second: Taxes are deferred on income and growth until you start taking distributions.

Third: Your employer may match some or all of your contributions. If your employer does offer a match, make sure you contribute at least enough to get the full match. Otherwise, it's like throwing free money away or leaving money on the table that could be helping you accumulate more money for retirement.

Please note that another option is the Roth 403(b) plan,[48] where growth is tax deferred but initial contributions are after taxes, and withdrawals in retirement are then tax free. (Roth Plans are discussed in Chapter 8.)

The three primary types of contributions are elective deferrals, nonelective contributions, and a combination of the two. Elective deferrals are made under a salary reduction agreement. The agreement allows the employer to withhold a worker's money from their paycheck and instead contribute it directly to their 403(b) account.

If it is a traditional 403(b) (as opposed to a Roth), you don't pay federal or state income taxes on this money until you take distributions (withdraw) from your account. If the contributions are to a Roth 403(b), you're taxed when you make your contribution, but qualified distributions are tax exempt—including any earnings.

The IRS also allows your employer to make contributions that are not part of a salary reduction agreement. These are nonelective contributions, and they include "salary match" agreements, discretionary contributions, and mandatory employer contributions. Ohio has joined many states in having moved toward a mix of elective and nonelective plans; for some of their workers, the employer contribution has become larger.

457 Plans

Since 1977, Ohio's state and local government employees have had the benefit of a supplemental retirement program administered with adherence to IRS code section 457.[49] This is a tax deferred, supplemental retirement income plan that is used to reduce taxes and secure retirement with an additional source of funds available when needed.

Similar to 401(k) plans offered in the private sector, the 457 is tax deferred, meaning the money comes out of your paycheck before taxes and goes straight into the account, where all growth is tax deferred. So your paycheck ends up being reduced by less than you'd expect because of the additional tax savings. When you retire and begin taking money out of the account (distributions), those withdrawals are taxed as ordinary income.

A 457 plan or, more accurately, a 457(b) plan, is like the more common 401(k) and 403(b) plan in that it offers state worker participants a defined contribution method to save for retirement. The plan sponsor provides you with a list of investment mutual funds, and you choose which ones your contributions are invested in. Other plans, like the one used by many municipalities, might also be actively managed.

One of the great benefits of a 457 plan is that if you leave your job or retire before age 59 1/2 and start withdrawing funds from a 457 plan, you will not be charged a penalty by the IRS (with 401[k] and 403[b] funds, that penalty is 10 percent). You will, however, still have to pay federal and state income taxes. 457 Roth plans may also be available. We discuss these further in Chapter 8.

Catch-Up Contributions

For 2020, the IRS allows individuals to save up to $19,500 per year in a 457 plan. Those over age 50 may also make annual "catch-up" contributions[50] of an additional $6,500. The 457 plan allows an enhanced catch-up provision over the other two plans mentioned, in that many qualify to contribute twice the annual limit, or $39,000, in 2020; the only stipulation is that you cannot contribute more than your salary. Learn more about catch-up contributions in Chapter 7 for a more detailed explanation of this unique benefit.

The next chapter will further define the current contribution limits; these maximum amounts are typically revised every three years.

SUMMARY: Chapter 6

- 403(b) plans are tax sheltered and possibly employer matched.
- 457 plans may offer "catch-up" options with no early withdrawal fees.

7

CONTRIBUTION
LIMITS

When you contribute to a retirement plan, it's important to remember that you are only *deferring* taxes on the amount you place in the acceptable plan(s). The agreement you're making with the Internal Revenue Service is that at some point in the future, you will retire and begin to take withdrawals from your retirement plan. These withdrawals will be taxed at the proper amount for your life situation at the time you choose to withdraw them.

One expected benefit of deferral is that you will pay less in taxes overall; chances are you'll be earning less income by that point and may consequently fall into a lower tax bracket. The second expected benefit is the pre-tax contributions from your pay will grow tax deferred, which will allow your money to grow much faster than if you tried to do the same thing in a non-retirement account where you had to pay taxes along the way.

A number of different retirement plan options may be available to you depending on where you have worked, whether or not you also own a business, and whether you have ever worked at a for-profit organization. If you have multiple retirement plans and have contributed to more than one during any given fiscal year, the aggregate amount saved cannot exceed the overall single limit for that respective plan type.

Here is a list of some retirement plans available today:

- 401(k)
- 403(b)
- 457(b)
- SIMPLE IRA plans
- Traditional IRA
- Roth IRA

Let's discuss the ways you can contribute to these types of accounts and their individual contribution limits.

Contribution Types And Methods

First, let's briefly examine the different contribution types.

Elective Deferral (Salary Contribution)

For those whose paycheck amounts vary due to overtime or other factors, elective deferral[51] is a good option. Individuals can choose to vary the amount of their contribution month to month. In most cases, plans permit the employee to specify a dollar amount, or percentage of their overall paycheck, to defer. Plans offering elective deferral may include 401(k), 403(b), 457, or SIMPLE IRA.

Catch-Up Contributions (Salary Contribution)

Participants who will be over the age of 50 by the end of the year may wish to opt for catch-up contributions,[52] which are a pre-tax contribution that you arrange with your employer. You typically can select a dollar amount or a percentage of overall pay. These deferral contributions are in addition to the usual maximum limit, and can be made each calendar year.

ROTH Contributions

These are elective contributions[53] that do not defer taxes in the tax year they are withheld; they are taxed as part of your gross income. However, upon distribution, you are not subject to income tax on the amount withdrawn. ROTH-type withholding can be allowed in 401(k), 403(b), and 457(b) plans.

Next, we'll look at specific types of contributions, their limits, and real-life examples.

Elective Deferral

The IRS has a set contribution limit for the amount of income (pre-tax and Roth) you are allowed to defer to 401(k), 403(b), and 457 plans: $19,500 (as of 2020, through at least 2021). An individual plan may have a lower limit; a lower salary may restrict you as well. You are permitted to have multiple retirement plans as desired, but this cumulative limit must not be exceeded; doing so may cause additional taxation and possible penalties.

Real-Life Scenario

You're 40 years old, and you have already deferred $3,500 for this year in pre-tax contributions to your employer's 403(b) plan. Then you change jobs and your new employer offers a 401(k) plan. Can you participate in that plan, too? You may, if that's allowed by the new plan. But because of the overall limit, the maximum you may defer to the new plan this fiscal year is $16,000 (remember the $19,500 individual limit, and $3,500 contributed to your previous employer's plan). Remember that the total amount deferred to *both plans* may not exceed your individual limit for that year.

Age 50-Plus Catch-Ups

If you will reach age 50 by December 31 in any given year, your individual limit for that year and going forward is increased by $6,500. In actual numbers, this increases your maximum annual allowable amount deferred to $26,000 across all plans ($19,500 + $6,500).

If your spouse works in the private sector and their 401(k) contributions are capped because of testing requirements, if they are age 50 or older, they can still contribute the additional $6,500 per year. This additional amount is outside of normal contribution caps; many people make the mistake of assuming if their employer says they can't contribute more than, say, 6 percent of their salary because of the testing rules, they also can't do the additional $6,500, but that is not correct.

Real-Life Scenario

You're 51 years old and have both a 401(k) and a 403(b) plan. Both allow contributions up to $19,500 annually. Because of your age, you can only contribute a combined total of $26,000 to your plans.

Tax Deferral Limited By Compensation

Individual plans may set lower limits, but most public service retirement plans in Ohio, at least, set their employee contribution limits at the maximum amounts allowed by the IRS. Under these limits, the most you can contribute to a plan is the lesser of:

- The allowed amount for that plan for the year, or
- All eligible and includible compensation defined by plan terms (compensation deferred in one plan cannot be included in another).

Many public service workers also own small businesses, which they work in during their off-hours. This self-employment allows for alternative tax deferment plans on net earnings from that business.

Real-Life Scenario

You are 54 years old, you work for the state of Ohio, and you participate in your employer's 403(b) retirement plan. Your maximum allowable deferred contribution rate for that plan is $26,000 for the year.

You also have a small side business, from which you make $8,500 anually. You may contribute an additional $26,000 to your 403(b) and $8,500 (100 percent) to a SIMPLE IRA plan. What you *cannot* do is contribute more than $8,500 (100 percent) to that SIMPLE IRA[54] plan.

403(b) Catch-Up Deferral Limits

In the tax year that you reach the age of 50, you are permitted to increase your annual deferrals to your 403(b) plan by as much as $3,000, but *only if* you've worked for the entity providing that plan for *at least* 15 years. This additional deferral is *separate* from the age 50 catch-up discussed earlier. If your plan is administered to allow both types, your annual allowed contributions are considered to be made first against the 15-year catch-up provision. Therefore, your total annual contributions may now be as high as $29,000.

Separate Limits For 457(b) Plan Participants

Take note here, because this is an area that many don't take full advantage of. If you are eligible for a 403(b), 401(k), or other deferral plan, *and* a 457(b) plan, you may be eligible for separate deferrals altogether. The amounts contributed and deferred here are not combined with what's put into your other plans.

Elective Deferrals: Starting in 2020, you may defer up to $19,500 to your plan annually, provided that doesn't exceed 100 percent of your pay from the employer sponsoring the plan. If catch-up contributions are allowed, you may also contribute under that provision without aggregating it with other plan limits.

Catch-Up Deferrals For 457(b): The governmental 457(b) plan may allow people age 50 and over to defer catch-up contributions of an additional $6,500 annually.

Catch-Up Deferral Special For 457(b): The governmental 457(b) plan may also allow a special "3-year catch-up" if you haven't put in the maximum allowable contribution in prior years. For example, if you are age 45 in 2020 and you contribute $16,000 to your 457(b) that year, in a future year you'll be allowed to contribute an additional $3,500 as a catch-up provision ($19,500 – $16,000 = $3,500). This special allowance, which can be done at any age, needs to be completed *before* you reach the plan's normal retirement age, as follows:

- In addition to the normal annual limit, you may also contribute amounts that were allowed but were not contributed in prior years.
- You may contribute double the allowed 457(b) limit (in 2020, $19,500 x 2 = $39,000).

If a 457(b) allows the age-50 catch-up at the same time as the 3-year catch-up, you may select the option that adds to the largest deferral. *You may not use both.*

Real-Life Scenario

You contribute to both a 457(b) and a 403(b) plan; they each allow the maximum deferral limit. These scenarios are permitted under IRS tax laws:

- Under age 50: $19,500 to each plan (as of 2020).
- Age 50 or older in a governmental 457(b) plan: $26,000 to each plan if both plans allow age-50 catch-ups ($6,500 additional).
- Age 50 or older in a nongovernmental 457(b) plan: $26,000 to the 403(b) plan; $19,500 to the 457(b) plan.
- Age 50 or over, with a 457(b) plan that has a 3-year catch-up: $26,000 to the 403(b) plan; $39,000 to the 457(b) plan ($19,500 x 2).
- If you've worked for a qualified organization for at least 15 years, you can defer up to an additional $3,000 to the 403(b) plan account.

If plan participants are making catch-up contributions to a retirement plan using elective deferrals, they cannot also make lump sum contributions. These catch-up contributions must be made before the end of the plan year and 100 percent must come from salary deferrals. Therefore, if you are thinking about doing this in any given year, it's better to get started as early as possible. Unless you have an extremely high salary, it's not smart to wait until December to make your salary deferrals in the last two pay periods of the year.

IRA Contributions

Contributions to a personal IRA (traditional or Roth) may be limited if you or your spouse are already covered by a retirement plan at work, and also, in some cases, if your income exceeds levels stipulated by the IRS.

IRA guidelines take into consideration whether you or your spouse already participates in a retirement plan at work. Roth IRA guidelines also have income considerations, which change periodically. Individuals who are age 50 or over at the end of the calendar year are allowed catch-up contributions. This deferred contribution is $1,000 above the standard $6,000 deferral limit.

The examples below will help spell out the rules.

Real-Life Scenarios

- A single student with part-time earnings of $3,500 in 2020 may contribute up to $3,500 (100 percent) to his IRA for the 2020 tax year. This contribution may also be made by someone other than the student (parent, grandparent, etc.).
- An employee making $5,500 with no employer-sponsored retirement plan may defer up to a combined $5,500 *total* across both a traditional IRA and a Roth IRA.
- Someone between the ages of 50 and 72 with no taxable income in 2020, who is married and whose spouse claims $60,000 on their joint tax return, may contribute $6,000, plus an additional $1,000 catch-up on their joint return. This catch-up amount is allowed after the age of 50.

Roth IRA Contribution Rules

The rules for contributions for a Roth IRA and a traditional IRA are very similar. The biggest difference is that your income and/or tax filing status may limit your ability to contribute to a Roth IRA. These income limits increase modestly every year, and can be found in the publication IRS 590-A.[55] These are the limits and phaseout dollar amounts as of 2020.

IRA Contributions For Age 72 And Above

With the passage of the Secure Act[56] in December of 2019, you are now able to make contributions to a traditional IRA even after the age of 72. Individuals may still make contributions to a Roth IRA as well. Roll-overs (including those from 403[b] and 401[k] plans) may be rolled into either a traditional or Roth IRA, no matter what your age.

Spousal IRAs

For those filing a joint tax return where one spouse had little or no taxable income, contributions may be made to an IRA for each person. If you file a joint return, you may be able to contribute to an IRA even if you did not have taxable compensation, as long as your spouse had some. The amount of your combined contributions can't be more than the taxable compensation reported on your joint return. This is a great way to maximize deferred savings for retirement, even if one or both of you do not have an employer-sponsored plan.

•   •   •

2020—Traditional IRA

Filing Status	Modified Adjusted Gross Income (MAGI)	Deduction Limit
Single Individuals	≤ $65,000	Full deduction up to the amount of your contribution limit
	> $65,000 but < $75,000	Partial deduction (calculate)
	≥ $75,000	No deduction
Married (filing joint returns)	≤ $104,000	Full deduction up to the amount of your contribution limit
	> $104,000 but < $124,000	Partial deduction (calculate)
	≥ $124,000	No deduction
Married (filing separately)	Not eligible	Full deduction up to the amount of your contribution limit
	< $10,000	Partial deduction
	≥ $10,000	No deduction
Nonactive participant spouse (i.e., those with spouses who earn no income)	≤ $196,000	Full deduction up to the amount of your contribution limit
	> $196,000 but < $206,000	Full deduction up to the amount of your contribution limit
	≥ $206,000	Full deduction up to the amount of your contribution limit

Table D

2020—ROTH IRA

Filing Status	Modified Adjusted Gross Income (MAGI)	Contribution Limit
Single Individuals	< $124,000	$6,000
	≥ $124,000 but < $139,000	Partial contribution (calculate)
	≥ $139,000	Not eligible
Married (filing joint returns)	< $196,000	$6,000
	≥ $196,000 but < $206,000	Partial contribution (calculate)
	≥ $206,000	Not eligible
Married (filing separately)	Not eligible	$6,000
	< $10,000	Partial contribution (calculate)
	≥ $10,000	Not eligible

Table E

If you have the option to choose one or more of many plans, you should consider the fees and flexibility of each different investment option so that you can maximize your deferred contributions. Even though traditional IRAs and Roth IRAs may give you more flexibility, you may also need to look to your employer-offered 457 or 403(b) plan to maximize your pre-tax contributions. This is especially important if your household income exceeds certain limits.

Employer Match

Another important tip: It's generally not a good idea to forfeit matched contributions from your employer. Many people don't contribute to their own plans up to the matching deferral percentage offered by their employer. This is often leaving money on the table. If the employer is matching dollar for dollar up to 6 percent, it's usually a good idea to contribute *at least* 6 percent of your salary to get that additional money.

We've discussed the guidelines for taking advantage of many different retirement plans while also possibly enhancing your tax situation. Maximizing these options may well require bringing in a professional, someone with plenty of experience who won't overlook the intricacies of your specific situation.

The Miracle Of Compound Growth

When it comes to retirement, the earlier you get started saving, the better. The sooner you get your money into some sort of tax deferred, interest-bearing account, the more money your money can make *for* you. This is the concept of compound growth, and there's a reason why many people call it a miracle.

Albert Einstein[57] was heard to say, "Compound interest is the eighth wonder of the world," and after 27 years of personal experience seeing its effects firsthand, I'm inclined to agree with him.

To illustrate just how powerful compound interest can be, here's a scenario for your consideration. Let's say you're making an annual contribution of about $2,600, or about $217 per month. That represents an 8 percent contribution each month. If you were to start contributing under these terms at the age of 25, and continued doing so for the next 10 years, and then stopped contributing altogether, how much money do you think your account would hold by retirement age? The answer is—drum roll—due to the magic of compound interest, at age 65, you'd have $470,333.

By contrast, if you started at age 35 and made that same monthly contribution for 30 years, you'd only have $346,355 at age 65. That's an overall difference of $124,000, which is huge.

It's important to keep in mind that, while compound interest can be powerful, it's not usually a straight line. Markets returns vary from year to year, sometimes higher, sometimes negative. But the goal is an average over time that gradually trends upward.

Consider the differences between the two approaches. For the second scenario, you're waiting 10 years, but contributing for three times longer overall (30 years instead of 10). By delaying those 10 years, you're paying three times as much of your own money, only to end up with an amount that is ultimately smaller.

This underscores the importance of starting early. If you waited until age 35 to start investing, you've saved yourself $26,000 in the short term, but sacrificed $124,000 in the long-term. Is that worth it? I think that most of us would agree that it isn't. Most people don't fully understand the numbers involved. These are the kinds of things that most of us should consider before it's too late.

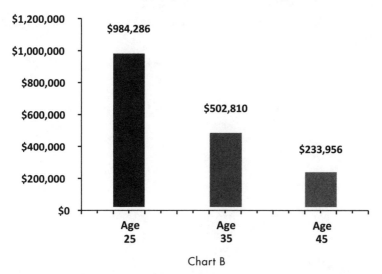

Chart B

This table demonstrates the importance of starting early. It assumes an annual investment of $6,000, assumes a steady 6 percent annual re-turn, starts from the ages of 25, 35, and 45, and assumes retirement at age 65.

This table demonstrates the importance of starting early. It assumes an annual investment of $6,000, assumes a steady 6 percent annual return, and starts from the ages of 25, 35, and 45.

SUMMARY: Chapter 7

- Consider investing the maximum amount you're allowed to in any and all tax deferred plans.
- If you're over 50 and just starting to save, find out how you can help make up for what you *weren't* investing in previous years.
- IRAs have different contribution rules for different situations; be sure you know what applies to you.
- Even if your spouse had no (or very limited) income, you might still be able to contribute to an IRA for them.
- If possible, invest the maximum amount that your employer is willing to match.
- Begin investing as early as possible to maximize your overall gains via compound return.

8

TRADITIONAL VERSUS ROTH RETIREMENT FUNDING

You most likely have Roth options in addition to traditional retirement savings plans, which add to the confusion of selecting which ones are best for you. On a simple level, the Roth style of 403(b), 401(k), or governmental 457(b) plans allows invested money to grow in a tax exempt status, and distributions are taken without tax consequence. Unlike a traditional deferral plan, your income is taxed *prior* to investing. This type of deferral has pros and cons, and in order to utilize it properly, you will need to forecast your needs until retirement, your earnings expected on these plans, and even how your tax rate may change after you stop working.

No one's "crystal ball" is sharp enough to know what will happen next year, let alone many years out, but with the right planning you can mix the two types of retirement plans for a blend that will hopefully meet your projected needs. To start, let's examine Roth plans more closely.

•　　•　　•

What Is A Designated Roth Contribution?

As mentioned earlier, traditional plans defer your contributions *before* taxes are applied—you pay taxes once you begin taking withdrawals in retirement. The Roth varieties of these plans, however, have you pay taxes *now* on the money you contribute. Because of this tax structure, having a Roth plan increases your reported gross income for the years you make your contributions, but lowers it for the years you make your withdrawals; a traditional plan works in the reverse.

The effect is that the IRS gets their cut up front, rather than when you withdraw or take qualified distributions later. A *qualified distribution* occurs either at least five years from the first contribution to your Roth plan OR after you reach age 59 1/2, whichever comes later. Additional qualified distribution scenarios include withdrawals due to disability or withdrawals to your beneficiary upon your death. Keep in mind, however, that the principal, your contributions, can come out at any time; it's any money gained through interest that has to be delayed.

Roth Plan Rollovers

If you plan on rolling over your traditionally funded 403(b), 457, or 401(k) to a Roth IRA in retirement in one lump sum, expect to pay a lot of money in taxes to the IRS in the year of conversion. This is where you will need a tax professional to sit down with you and make sure you are making the right decision. A move like this could easily push you into a higher tax bracket, cause Medicare premiums to go up (if you are over age 65), and could have many other implications.

Sometimes, it makes more sense to roll the money over to a traditional IRA and then gradually convert some of the money to a Roth IRA over several years, which will reduce tax and other consequences. When we look at this idea for our clients, I have our accountant do some income tax projections so the clients clearly understand the pros and cons of the different ways of implementing this strategy. Having money in a Roth is a great retirement move, but it's important to make sure any large rollovers are done in the most prudent manner possible.

Roth IRA

The Roth IRA was first presented as a retirement plan option as part of the 1997 Taxpayer Relief Act. The name "Roth" does not come from an acronym or a particular section of legal code, but instead from Delaware senator William Roth,[58] its chief legislative sponsor. This type of IRA has many similarities to the traditional IRA, including contribution limits.

Similarities aside, a Roth IRA is distinct from the traditional IRA because of how it is taxed. Traditional IRA contributions are made with pre-tax dollars, which are taxed upon withdrawal. Roth IRA contributions are made on money that has *already* been taxed. The benefit to the investor is the distributions, including any earnings, and they are exempt from taxation.

An additional benefit is that there are no required distributions from a Roth IRA—you don't have to start taking money from it just because you reach a certain life stage.

Permitted dollar amounts will change over time; you're Financial Quarterback or the IRS can keep you apprised of the most up-to-date information.

The IRS has established income limits, both maximums and minimums, for Roth accounts. Traditional IRAs do not have maximum earnings limits. You can refer back to Chapter 7 for details on minimums and when there are maximum income requirements for contribution limits.

Roth plans also have a maximum salary, which limits high-income households. The amounts are adjusted each year; see the IRS for the most recent numbers. As an example, in 2020, a married couple with adjusted gross income less than $196,000 may make full Roth IRA contributions; the upper adjusted gross income limit before the phase-out starts, per the IRS, for a single person contributing, is $124,000.

Features	Traditional IRA	Roth IRA
Who can contribute?	You can contribute if you (or your spouse, if filing jointly) have taxable compensation.	You can contribute at any age if you (or your spouse, if filing jointly) have taxable compensation and your modified adjusted gross income is below certain amounts.
Are my contributions deductible?	Can deduct contributions if you qualify.	Contributions aren't deductible.
How much can I contribute?	The most you can contribute to **all** of your traditional and Roth IRAs is the smaller of: • $6,000 for 2020; $7,000 if you're age 50 or older by the end of the year; or • Your taxable compensation for the year.	
What is the deadline to make contributions?	Your tax return filing deadline (not including extensions). For example, you can make 2020 IRA contributions until April 15, 2021.	
When can I withdraw money?	Money can be withdrawn anytime.	
Do I have to take required minimum distributions?	Must start taking distributions by April 1 following the year in which you turn age 72, and by December 31 of later years.	Not required if you are the original owner.
Are my withdrawals and distributions taxable?	Any deductible contributions and earnings you withdraw or that are distributed from your traditional IRA are taxable. Also, if you are under age 59½, you may have to pay an additional 10% tax for early withdrawals unless you qualify for an exception.	None, if it's a qualified distribution (or a withdrawal that is a qualified distribution). Otherwise, part of the distribution or withdrawal may be taxable. If you are under age 59½, you may also have to pay an additional 10% tax for early withdrawals unless you qualify for an exception.

Table F

Deciding Which Plan Is Best

Deciding upon a traditional plan, a Roth, or both requires making assumptions about your future, and even taking the time to thoroughly analyze potential scenarios. Some of these scenarios you have control over; others, you don't.

Roth 401(k), 403(b), IRAs Versus Traditional			
	Roth 401(k)	Roth IRA	Pre-Tax 401(k)
Contributions	Designated Roth employee elective contributions are made with *after-tax dollars*.	Roth IRA contributions are made with *after-tax dollars*.	Traditional employee elective contributions are made with *before-tax dollars*.
Income Limits	No income limit to participate.	Income limits: •2020-modified AGI married $206,000 single $139,000	No income limitation to participate.
Maximum Elective Contribution	*Aggregate** employee elective contributions limited to $19,500 in 2020; (plus an additional $6,500 for employees age 50 or over).	Contribution limited to $6,000 plus an additional $1,000 for employees age 50 or over in 2020.	Same aggregate* limit as Roth 401(k).
Taxation of Withdrawals	Withdrawals of contributions and earnings are not taxed, provided it's a qualified distribution—the account has been held at least 5 years and withdrawals are made: • On account of disability, • On or after death, or • On or after age 59½.	Same as Roth 401(k); can have a qualified distribution for a first-time home purchase.	Withdrawals are subject to federal and most state income taxes.
Required Distributions	Distributions must begin no later than age 72, unless still working and not a 5% owner.	No requirement to start taking distributions while owner is alive.	Same as Roth 401(k).
*This limitation is by individual, rather than by plan. You can split annual deferrals elective between designated Roth contributions and traditional pre-tax contributions, but your combined contributions cannot exceed the overall deferral limit. Adapted from site.			

Table G

If you're young and have many years to go until retirement, it may make sense to allocate more of your retirement savings to a Roth account; the assumption here is that the same amount of money invested will become greater over a longer period when you do not have to pay tax on the distributions in retirement. The downside to this is that the same amount of money invested will cost you more because it is taxed first. Oftentimes, younger people often need the money *now*, for living expenses and saving for home ownership and raising children. If regular living expenses may interfere with your long-term savings goals, find the money to at least go the traditional route; *any* savings are better than no savings at all.

Another consideration, which is completely out of your hands, is what income tax rates will be at the time when you retire and begin taking withdrawals. Conventional wisdom says tax rates trend upwards over time; conventional wisdom also suggests you'll make less overall in retirement than during your working years, which will lower your tax bracket.

The further away you are from retirement, the more difficult it is to forecast the future in terms of your retirement tax bracket and what actual tax rates will be. I like to work through different scenarios with my clients and run the numbers to see how they will fare. Which set of circumstances are the most favorable for this person's individual circumstances? Examining different scenarios often leads to leaning more toward one type of retirement fund over the other. In most cases, clients place some money in each type of account; some opt to place more in Roth accounts, while others feel safer deferring taxes by contributing a greater share of their savings to a traditional fund for now.

If you are age 72 or older, you are required to take distributions out of your traditional plans, or else face severe monetary penalties. This is *not* the case for Roth accounts.

Many who have retired from public service careers find their normal pension to be ample for day-to-day living expenses. Those people can benefit from leaving other money to continue growing in a tax exempt account. This money can then be used when retirees have large expenses such as buying a new car or replacing the roof on their house.

Roth Plans As Inheritance

And if that money ends up being unneeded, it will continue to grow until it can be passed on as an inheritance. If this is your intention, be sure to assign a beneficiary. The Roth IRA will pass to your beneficiaries tax free as long as you have owned it for more than five years. The beneficiaries may then take distributions even if they are not of retirement age themselves. Early distributions can be a significant plus for this type of account.

Both traditional plans and Roth plans can avoid the unnecessary court costs and hassles of probate (we'll talk about this in Chapter 12) if the proper beneficiary designations are made. When you bequeath an IRA of either type to an heir other than your spouse, they will be required to take scheduled withdrawals each year. These distributions will be taxable to your heirs under the traditional plan and tax exempt for Roth beneficiaries.

Early Withdrawals: Friend Or Foe?

One of the biggest benefits of a Roth plan can also be one of its primary drawbacks, early withdrawals. You may withdraw your contribution to a Roth IRA penalty free at any time for any reason, but the gains have to stay until after you reach at least age 59 1/2 or have owned the account for at least five years, whichever is greater. Money that was converted into a Roth IRA cannot be taken out penalty free until at least five years after the conversion.

By contrast, for traditional plans, you must be over age 59 1/2 for any withdrawals. There are a few exceptions. One is that if you're a first-time home buyer, you also have the option of withdrawing up to $10,000 early from either plan, although you'll pay income taxes on any amount withdrawn from the traditional plan in order to avoid a further IRS penalty.

The downside to the flexibility of the Roth is that it is very tempting to use those funds for things other than retirement. Retirement planning falls apart without discipline. If you question whether you can maintain the necessarily discipline to not spend your retirement savings for nonretirement things, you may wish to consider allocating more of your funds to traditional deferred income savings plans.

As is the case for life in general, none of us know what the future will bring. When deciding between Roth funds, traditional funds, or a combination of both, you should estimate your potential future tax rate relative to your current rate, and also consider how much time this money will be invested to compound and grow. And as you get older, you may also wish to review who will inherit these accounts if you don't use them, and how it will affect their financial position.

SUMMARY: Chapter 8

- Roth-style 403(b), 401(k), or 457(b) retirement accounts allow accumulations to grow exempt from tax. Contributions to Roth programs are *after* you have paid taxes.
- Deciding between Roth plans or traditional qualified plans requires analyzing scenarios developed by "best-guess" assumptions about the future.
- With proper planning, a Roth fund can easily be passed on to your descendants. Be sure to select a beneficiary on all your retirement accounts.
- Think carefully before withdrawing early. Earlier access to your money can be beneficial or detrimental; be sure you're not tempted to spend the money frivolously.

9

MAKING THE MOST OF SERVICE CREDITS

Government employees in Ohio who participate in pension programs may purchase what is called *service credit* in order to increase future pension payments or to reduce the amount of time left until they can retire. This credit can be purchased for specific types of prior employment, or even for leaves of absence. If you worked in a job covered by a different public pension than you're currently under (like OPERS, STRS, SERS, or OP&F), if you worked for the federal government, or even if you served in the military, you may be eligible to buy back that time and add it to your existing years of service. Did you work in another state? Or even have an absence due to pregnancy? This time might also be eligible to be purchased.

In this chapter, we'll discuss service, the impact of a proper service credit strategy, how your defined benefit plan provides this benefit, and how you can use it to your advantage.

●   ●   ●

The Impact Of Service Credits

On a basic level, purchasing service credits can do one of three things to your public service retirement plan:

- **Increase your overall retirement pay.** If you have already satisfied the years of service requirement for a full retirement benefit without purchasing credit, you may be able to purchase additional credit to *increase* the size of that benefit. For example, for every year of service you purchase, you might be able to increase your monthly pension by an additional 2.2 percent.
- **Reduce or eliminate an early retirement shortfall.** If you retire early, you are not typically eligible for full retirement benefits. By purchasing service credits, you may be able to bring yourself closer to full benefits.
- **Allow eligibility for some retirement benefits.** If you started your career in the system late and are not yet eligible for a pension, or you would like to retire earlier than naturally permitted, purchasing time may allow you to retire earlier.

The liability to your pension plan increases for any time purchased. The cost to you is determined based on your age and years of service. The closer you are to retirement now, the higher your cost may be.

Service Credit Eligibility

Start by determining if you are allowed to purchase service credit. Are there eligible periods of time in your work history for which you can purchase credit?

The first step is reaching out to your human resources department and having them certify your time. Certifying time does not create any obligations. Once certified, HR, or the specific agency that you are buying back the time from, can provide a copy of a cost statement, which will tell you the types of purchasable credit you're entitled to and how much that credit would cost.

Next, make an appointment with your benefits counselor, and then your Financial Quarterback. Together, you will look at what you're able to purchase and figure out the best course of action. You are typically allowed to purchase one year of service credit for each eligible year of absence.

Real-Life Scenario

You are a police officer currently invested in the OP&F retirement plan, but you spent four years in the military prior to joining the department. You may be eligible to purchase these four years as service credits and add them to your OP&F pension, which could possibly make you eligible for DROP and other benefits sooner than expected.

How Should You Pay For Service Credits?

If you are eligible to purchase service credits, should you? How do you know if it is worthwhile? That depends on your individual circumstances. When considering service credits, you must think about where the money to purchase them will come from and balance any potential risks against the expected benefits.

As discussed previously, most pension managers estimate a return of 7.5 to 8 percent in their calculations. As the reality of these projections may be questionable, it's advisable to use an even lower percentage; we suggest 6.5 percent, for your individual analysis.

It is not recommended that you take out a loan (borrow money) in order to increase your future pension amount. Your employer likely has an installment method that allows you to take additional money out of your salary in order to purchase service credits, and so long as you're more than five years away from retirement, it's smarter to use this installment method than it would be to borrow money against your home or another credit line.

One of the more favorable ways to purchase prior years of service is with pre-tax money by using your 403(b) account, 457, or even an IRA. Money can be transferred from these plans directly to the pension, eliminating any income tax considerations. Just make sure you never touch the money yourself; doing so would make it a taxable event.

If you are considering using either an IRA or other qualified deferred money to purchase service credits, compare the IRA's expected return to the boost your pension would see from buying them, and then factor in the normal contractual guarantees of your pension. This will help you to determine if utilizing deferred money is the best decision in this situation.

Tip: You may use funds from any non-Roth IRA, and possibly your 403(b) or 457, to purchase additional years if eligible. When the purchase itself is a nontaxable event, it's always better to use pre-tax money than after-tax.

When To Purchase

You may purchase service credits up to three months *after* you retire, but it's strongly suggested that you opt to buy back years of service PRIOR to your actual retirement. The longer you wait, the higher the cost of buying those service years. You should also weigh the cost of purchase against the risk associated with buying credit. One risk is that any money used to buy service credits could be partially or fully lost should you die before or in early retirement. Another risk is that you may wind up working longer than previously expected; in that case, the benefit of buying additional service credits could be reduced.

Another important consideration—buying additional service years to increase your pension payout may— also serve to *reduce* your Social Security benefits. Sometimes you can also simply transfer credits from one pension system to another without adding any money out of your pocket.

It's important to consider these provisions before purchasing service credits, as doing so can have unforeseen financial consequences.

SUMMARY: Chapter 9

- Service credits can increase your retirement pay, reduce a retirement budget shortfall, or even allow you to be eligible for benefits you might otherwise not qualify for.
- Speak to your job's current benefits counselor and prior employer to determine whether you are eligible to purchase service credits and how much they will cost.
- Try to use pre-tax money from deferred accounts whenever possible, or consider using your plan's installment method for buying up the pension payout.
- Take previous, current, and future interest rates into account when deciding when to purchase.
- Increasing pension payments via service credits may *decrease* Social Security benefits.

10

THE RULES: SOCIAL SECURITY AND YOUR PENSION

O hio civil employees that participate in STRS, SERS, OPERS, OP&F, or HPRS need to fully understand how Social Security works with their particular pension plan.

Social Security doesn't work for pensioners the same way it works for those who have worked in the private sector. Pensioners have a very real possibility of lower future Social Security benefits as a result of current pension earnings. Many people find the rules for collecting both a pension from state pensions and Social Security benefits at the same time very confusing.

Understanding The Rules

The first thing to understand is that if you don't pay into 40 quarters of Social Security, you will pay substantially higher rates for Medicare Parts A and B.

To be eligible for **Social Security** retirement benefits, a worker born after 1928 must have accumulated at least 40 **quarters** of work in "covered employment." A "**quarter** of coverage" generally means the three-month calendar **quarter**. In addition, you must earn at least $1,410 in each **quarter** (as of 2020) for it to count.

The second thing you need to understand, as a participant in an Ohio pension plan, is that there are two provisions that can affect your Social Security payouts. They are called The Windfall Elimination Provision (WEP)[59] and the Government Pension Offset (GPO).

Windfall Elimination Provision (WEP)

The calculation of your Social Security benefits, including retirement and disability, can be affected by your government pension. Here's the reason, according to the Social Security Administration:

Rather than view payments from your pension as a low income and then base Social Security on previous contributions to the system, Congress decided instead to reduce, but not completely eliminate, the Social Security benefit. This is intended to create an equivalency to those who have paid into the system for longer, and to avoid what may be considered "double dipping" into retirement benefits.

The Social Security Administration determines an individual's benefit based on their earnings. Interestingly, benefits are weighed more heavily to those who have lower earnings overall (it is, after all, *Social Security*). The Windfall Elimination Provision (WEP) was added to the Social Security Act as an amendment in 1983. The WEP is intended to prevent government employees who receive a pension and did not pay into Social Security from receiving a larger monthly benefit the way a long-term, low-wage worker might.

WEP was designed to even out Social Security benefits (those with pensions in addition to Social Security) to what they'd have received if all of their earnings were in the Social Security system. Is this fair? Regardless of any individual's personal view on the matter, the fact is that the WEP isn't going away. Individuals need to understand how it will affect them and work within the provision.

Windfall Elimination Provision			
Year	Substantial earnings	Years of substantial earnings	Percentage
1987	$8,175	30 or more	90 percent
1988	$8,400	29	85 percent
1989	$8,925	28	80 percent
1990	$9,525	27	75 percent
1991	$9,900	26	70 percent
1992	$10,350	25	65 percent
1993	$10,725	24	60 percent
1994	$11,250	23	55 percent
1995	$11,325	22	50 percent
1996	$11,625	21	45 percent
1997	$12,150	20 or less	40 percent
1998	$12,675		
1999	$13,425		
2000	$14,175		
2001	$14,925		
2002	$15,750		
2003	$16,125		
2004	$16,275		
2005	$16,725		
2006	$17,475		
2007	$18,150		
2008	$18,975		
2009–2011	$19,800		
2012	$20,475		
2013	$21,075		
2014	$21,750		
2015–2016	$22,050		
2017	$23,625		
2018	$23,850		
2019	$24,675		
2020	$25,575		

Table H

Table H can help you determine what percentage of a payout you can expect based on how many years you have received a substantial income. The WEP only applies to *your* benefits; it is not applied to spousal or survivor benefits.

Real-Life Scenario

A patrol officer makes $50,000 per year in her day job. As a state employee, she does not pay into Social Security. However, she also works as a part-time employee in her husband's business; her annual pay there is about $6,000 annually, and the Federal Insurance Contributions Act payroll tax (FICA) is withheld.

When she retires, her part-time job history and previous Social Security withholdings would have suggested she is a low-earning person and entitled to a higher percentage of earnings as a Social Security beneficiary. In truth, if all her pay from both jobs were FICA earnings, the additional $6,000 in annual pay from the part-time job might not have contributed very much to a higher percentage Social Security payout.

The WEP adjusts for her actual work history and lowers her Social Security Payments accordingly. If the part-time job yielded her 30 years of substantial earnings (see Table H for minimum income required in each year) before she retires, she wouldn't have any reduction in Social Security. This is rare, but we have had several clients who worked long term in the private sector before joining a governmental agency, and they have been able to keep 100 percent of their pension benefits.

The WEP In Action

Now we'll discuss the WEP in more depth. If you have worked and paid into Social Security but also have a pension from work where you did *not* pay in (i.e., non-covered work), you will be affected by the WEP. Here are the basic mechanics public pension participants need to know:

- The highest amount that Social Security can be reduced will never exceed half of the pension amount. For 2020, the reduction amount is capped at $480.
- If you have over 20 years of paying into Social Security, (covered earnings) the reduction is reduced; after 30 years of covered employment, WEP doesn't apply at all.

Years Of Significant Earnings	Maximum Applied WEP Reduction
20 or Fewer	$480.00
21	$432.00
22	$384.00
23	$336.00
24	$288.00
25	$240.00
26	$192.00
27	$144.00
28	$96.00
29	$48.00
30+	$0

Table I

Real-Life Scenario

It is not uncommon for public workers to have had careers in the private sector for a period before starting their non-covered job. This creates the need for creative solutions to avoid a rule that can have very expensive consequences.

Adrianna had worked in marketing for 25 years before becoming a Communications Supervisor for the local county. As she was planning her retirement from her county position, she sought advice on when to begin to take Social Security. Adrianna was thinking about "keeping busy" with a part-time job rather than a complete retirement. We told her that if she started Social Security at her current age, her benefit would be reduced by $240 a month. *Forever.* She decided that she should hold off taking Social Security until she figured out exactly what she wanted to do.

A few weeks later, she was offered a part-time position. Together with our help, we were able to determine how every year of working at this position would increase her future Social Security payments. She discovered that if she worked for five more years and made more than the "substantial earning" amount each year ($25,575 for 2020), her future Social Security payments would not be reduced at all (see substantial earnings section earlier in this chapter).

Five years later, Adrianna is now deciding if she should leave the part-time job. By working just a few more years, she has increased her monthly Social Security benefit for the rest of her life.

Government Pension Offset (GPO)

The Government Pension Offset (GPO)[60] applies to spousal or surviving spouse Social Security benefits. It reduces an individual's Social Security payments if their spouse is also receiving payments from a government pension. The logic is similar to WEP in that it is intended to ensure that Social Security is distributed as a *social* safety net and will not enrich anyone unintentionally. The GPO provision affects many public service employees who are covered by an earnings-based pension.

Under the GPO, Social Security spousal or survivor benefits will be reduced by $2 for every $3 received from a government pension.

Please note: On your regular Social Security statements, the Personal Earnings and Benefit Estimate Statement (PEBES) will *not* provide information about the impact of the GPO on your future benefits. The PEBES[61] of your spouse will provide the Social Security dollar amounts to be reduced based on the amount of pension *you* are receiving.

The GPO In Action

To determine precisely how the GPO will affect *your spouse's* payments, multiply *your* annual pension amount by 0.66, and subtract that result from *their* annual Social Security benefit amount. The result, so long as it's not less than zero, is what you can expect to receive.

Real-Life Scenario

Katie worked in the County Clerk's office for 30 years, where she did not pay into Social Security. Her husband, Dave, was an attorney; he paid the maximum amount of Social Security taxes every year.

Dave had retired a few years earlier and is collecting $2,700 every month from Social Security. They are both eager to give their home a long overdue makeover. Six months after Katie joins Dave in retirement, Dave falls from the roof while putting a cap on the chimney. He doesn't survive his injuries.

Katie never paid into Social Security herself. Under GPO, she is not entitled to the full amount of Dave's Social Security as a survivor benefit. She will now collect Social Security reduced by 66 percent of her government pension.

Here is exactly how it works out in Katie and Dave's case:

Government Pension Offset (GPO) Reduction Formula	
$3,400	Katie's pension payment
X .66%	Calculate 66% of that payment
$2,244	The reduction to survivor's Social Security benefit
In Application	
$2,700	Dave's monthly Social Security benefit
-2,244	GPO Reduction
$456	Social Security benefit Katie will receive monthly

Table J

It is important to plan for the potential of this happening. It becomes even more important if the spouse receiving Social Security is in ill health.

Estimating Your GPO–Social Security Offset

Imagine you receive a government pension that pays $1,500 per month. Imagine you're also eligible for a Social Security spousal benefit of $700 per month.

Calculate the GPO by multiplying your monthly pension payment by 0.66: $1,500 x 0.66 = $990. Since that $990 is higher than the spousal Social Security benefit of $700, the spousal benefit would be eliminated entirely.

SUMMARY: Chapter 10

- Know the rules about WEP and GPO. There is no substitute for knowing the right information or seeking advice from retirement professionals that do.
- The WEP may reduce Social Security payments for those who have worked any amount of time in a nongovernmental job but who are also eligible for a government pension.
- If you receive a government pension, the GPO reduces the Social Security benefits of your spouse (or widow).

11

CHOOSING THE RIGHT PENSION PAYOUT

A s you plan for your future retirement, you'll be making many decisions based on unknown factors. You'll be trying to predict future expectations based on current needs. And these predictions—and the decisions you base off of them—will become more important than ever.

Many of the decisions you will have to eventually make are irreversible. They will affect you and your family for the rest of your life and possibly beyond. Making these decisions is a daunting task, and in this chapter we'll address many of the questions that will come up in the decision-making process. The following pages contain information that will reduce the mystery surrounding these decisions and the factors you should consider in order to make the best judgments.

Considerations And Options

When planning your retirement, here are some of the biggest issues to consider:

- Expected recurring financial obligations (rent/mortgage, monthly bills).
- Occasional big-ticket obligations (new car, family vacation).
- Social Security benefits (when to begin collecting).
- Health status (chronic conditions, major illnesses, disabilities).
- Healthcare insurance (to bridge the gap until you are eligible for Medicare at age 65).
- Spousal obligations.
- Current liabilities.
- Other available financial resources.
- Part-time or consulting opportunities.
- Long-term care needs.
- Bucket list items.

In the weeks leading up to your actual retirement, you'll be expected to determine your payout plan. In this chapter, we'll focus on the options and decisions you'll have to make regarding survivors (we'll discuss lump sum or partial lump sum distributions in depth starting in Chapter 13).

If you are married, your spouse may be required to execute a consent form when finalizing your monthly pension payout. Legally, pensions and retirement funds are considered joint property within a marriage. In some cases, a situation surrounding a previous or current marriage may require, under court order, for you to provide a continuing monthly benefit to someone. It is common to have the amounts payable under court order funded and planned for. These obligations must be made available during the lifetime of the beneficiary.

There are four basic options to consider (depending on your pension):

- Plan I — Single Life Annuity (SLA).
- Plan II — Joint and Survivor Annuity (JSA).
- Plan III — Life Annuity Certain and Continuous (LACC).
- Plan IV — Multiple Beneficiary Annuity (MBA).

Your retirement plan can likely offer benefit tables and calculators to help you weigh the differences in your individual situation. However, it's smart to speak directly with your employer's (or your pension's) benefits counselor to calculate the specific amounts you will receive under each option. The benefits counselor can also provide you with start dates, amounts contributed throughout your employment, and other information you might be missing. It's important to get the correct numbers so that you'll be making informed decisions.

Next, we'll discuss the plans available in more depth.

Plan I—Single Life Annuity (SLA)

The Single Life Annuity (SLA)[62] option provides maximum monthly benefits for the duration of your lifetime. However, the payments end at the time of your passing; there are no ongoing payments to any of your survivors. If the payments you have received do not exceed your overall contributions, *this* amount will be paid to your beneficiaries. In most cases, all the money you have personally contributed will have been exhausted by your monthly payments within the first two to three years of your retirement.

Please note: If you have selected SLA and then you opt to get married in retirement, this status change might permit you to change your selection to Plan II (Joint and Survivor Annuity). However, the window to make this change is usually only open for one year from the date on your marriage certificate. And marriage is the only time you are allowed to change from the Single Life Annuity option after retiring. The effective date of the new joint benefit amount to be paid is the date the application is received by your plan. The revised payments will begin on the first day of the following month.

Plan II—Joint And Survivor Annuity (JSA)

This plan provides a monthly benefit to you for the duration of your lifetime, and after you pass, your beneficiary(s) will continue to receive monthly payments for the rest of *their* lifetime(s). The amount you receive every month in this plan will be less than it would be under the Single Life option.

Under the Joint and Survivor Pension Annuity,[63] there are basically three subcategories to choose from:

Selection 1: Upon passing, your primary beneficiary receives the same monthly payment you had been receiving.

Selection 2: Upon your passing, your primary beneficiary receives half the previous monthly benefit you had been receiving.

Selection 3: Upon your passing, your primary beneficiary receives a specific dollar amount or percentage that you had previously designated. This designated amount must be more than $50 per month.

You will have to make a number of projections related to future expenses, non-pension earnings, and potential longevity to determine which option seems best suited to your circumstances.

Now that we've gone over the basic options, let's get back to additional considerations for a winning strategy.

Joint And Survivor Annuity With Reversion

This choice allows you to revert to the SLA plan under two different circumstances:

- Your primary beneficiary passes away before you do. The effective date of your new benefit amount is the first day of the month following your primary beneficiary's death.
- Your marriage to your primary beneficiary ends. You must obtain written consent from your former spouse or beneficiary or a copy of the official court documentation that authorizes reversion. The pension annuity will revert to either the date the application is received by your state plan

administrator or the date of divorce or annulment, whichever is later. The new benefit amount is paid beginning the first of the following month.

If JSA with reversion is selected and a non-spouse is named as beneficiary at retirement, and then you later get married, you will have the option of selecting your spouse as the new beneficiary within the first year of your marriage.

Joint And Survivor Annuity Without Reversion

Just as having a reversion allows you to revert back to SLA, choosing to go without reversion prohibits that. You will maintain your payments at the JSA level even if your beneficiary passes before you or your marriage to the beneficiary ends.

The biggest reason people will opt out of the reversion option is because going without provides incrementally more income for the retiree to live on (when compared to having the option for reversion).

It's important to have a handle on your expected costs in order to select which reversion method is best in your situation. If there is no reason to select the *with reversion* option, you are cutting yourself short of benefit payments each month.

Please note: *Not all plans offer this option.*

Plan III—Life Annuity Certain And Continuous (LACC)

The Life Annuity Certain and Continuous (LACC)[64] plan establishes a monthly benefit for the duration of your lifetime. Your beneficiary also receives benefits for a specified number of years from your retirement date. The period you choose is set by you, but is usually limited to between 5 and 20 years. If you pass away prior to the end of the guaranteed period, your beneficiary will receive the same monthly benefit until the period selected ends. If more than one person is named as your beneficiary, a lump sum payment equivalent to the present value of the remaining payments is evenly split between the beneficiaries.

The beneficiary in this plan may be a charity, trust, or church. In these cases, the value of expected future payments is added together, and the beneficiary receives one lump sum.

It is important to note that if you select LACC upon retiring, your payments are set and *cannot* change. This choice does, however, allow for a change of beneficiary with an identical guaranteed period end date.

Plan IV—Multiple Beneficiary Annuity (MBA)

You may choose (or be required) to provide lifetime benefits for up to four primary beneficiaries under a JSA plan. For each beneficiary, **you** have the option of either specifying a percentage of your total benefit or a flat dollar amount. You may not provide less than 10 percent (as either a flat rate or a percentage) unless directed by a court order. If a beneficiary is not your spouse, certain IRS limits to its designation may apply to the percent allowed.

When you pass away, monthly benefits are paid to the beneficiaries you designated at the time of retirement. If one of your beneficiaries predeceases you, it is imperative that you contact your plan administrator so that your plan benefits can be adjusted accordingly, as well as to avoid any legal confusion should you also pass away soon after. Doing this won't change the amounts payable to your other beneficiaries.

If you have chosen multiple primary beneficiaries, there are only two situations that enable you to change their payments after their initial designation.

- One of the primary beneficiaries is your spouse, and your marriage ends. You must have written consent from your former spouse or an official court order authorizing the change. The change is effective either on the date the application is received by the plan administrator or the date of the divorce, whichever comes latest. The new benefit amount is paid the first of the following month.

- Your primary beneficiaries are non-spouses and you get married after retiring. Within your first year of marriage, you may elect to change your plan to include your new spouse as a beneficiary. You may retain up to three beneficiaries you named when you retired (up to four beneficiaries total, the maximum allowed). The total combined monthly benefit payable to all your beneficiaries (if you pass away) cannot exceed the monthly benefit paid to you in life.

Spousal Considerations

If you are married, your spouse must consent to most of these payout options in writing.

Without spousal consent, most pensions will force you to receive a JSA with one-half going to the spouse (with reversion).

In certain situations, spousal consent is not required:

- You are required to elect a plan of payment following a court order, and your current spouse is also a beneficiary under that plan.
- You are required to provide an amount to one or more former spouses following a court order, and that amount is the maximum amount payable in a Joint and Survivor Annuity plan of payment.

Pairing Your Pension With Life Insurance

One planning strategy that may make mathematical sense is to opt for SLA and buy life insurance prior to retirement. The non-pensioned spouse is named beneficiary of the insurance. Doing this increases the monthly income from the pension plan while at the same time protecting the spouse should the pension owner predecease them.

The cost-effectiveness of this depends on the age and health of the individual for which life insurance is being sought and the unknown of how long each will live. However, life insurance companies have modified their policies for this specific type of planning, sometimes called a pension max.[65] You can now get life insurance with premium guarantees to age 100 or even 120.

This way you can have a guaranteed, known payment that will remain at that level so that, whenever you pass, the benefits will transfer tax free to your spouse. This allows you to have a higher monthly income from your SLA (instead of a lower monthly payout from a JSA) while you are living while also making sure your spouse is well taken care of when you pass.

If your pension also has a cost of living benefit (COLA), this strategy is even more important to you because your COLA increase each year will be based on your higher SLA payments, and therefore can add up to a considerable amount of money over time.

Changing Your Plan

You select your pension payout plan upon retirement. Once selected, the opportunity to change to a different plan depends on which one you originally selected. The opportunity to change is allowed under certain circumstances.

Single Life Annuity

If you choose a SLA plan at retirement and later marry, you may change your plan to a JSA and name your new spouse as beneficiary. You have one year from the date of the marriage license to do this. The application to change must be accompanied by a copy of your marriage certificate. The JSA option becomes effective on the date the application is received by your pension system. The new benefit amount will be paid beginning on the first of the following month.

Joint And Survivor Annuity With Reversion

You may revert to the SLA plan from a JSA plan under certain circumstances:

- **Your beneficiary predeceases you.** A copy of their death certificate must accompany your application to revert to SLA. The effective date of the revised benefit amount for SLA is the first day of the month following the date of death.
- **Your marriage to the beneficiary terminates.** This requires either consent from the former spouse or court documents demonstrating the change of ownership rights. The new selection is effective on either the date the application is received by your pension system or the date of divorce, whichever is latest. The revised benefit amount is paid beginning the first of the following month.

If JSA with reversion is selected and a non-spouse is named at retirement, and then you later get married, you will have the option of selecting your new spouse as the beneficiary. This change must be completed within the first year of your marriage.

Joint And Survivor Annuity Without Reversion

If you select JSA *without* reversion, you will never be able to revert to SLA. Under no circumstances can the plan, the payment method, or the primary beneficiary be altered.

Life Annuity Certain And Continuous

If you choose the LACC plan at retirement, you cannot change to a different plan after retirement. However, you do have the option to name a different beneficiary during the remaining years of the guaranteed period.

Withdrawal Option

When you terminate your position, you may elect to withdraw from your retirement account (this is not usually recommended unless your years of service are very low). This is not a type of retirement but the equivalent of taking qualified money from one account to place in another qualified account. The amount available will be the total amount you contributed, including service credit purchases.

Spousal Consent For Account Withdrawal

Most pension accounts are co-owned by you and your spouse. Any changes to beneficiaries or withdrawals must be accompanied by either a notarized form signed by your spouse or a court order specifying changed ownership rights.

Withdrawal Amount

The withdrawal amount will include the total of your personal contributions plus any additional amount payable under Section 3307.563 of the Revised Code.[66] The additional amount is determined by years of qualifying service credit and the interest rates set by the Retirement Board.

- With five or more years of qualifying service credit, an applied interest rate of 6 percent or less (compounded annually) will be paid on contributions along with an amount equal to 50 percent of the sum of your member contributions. Interest is also paid.
- With three to five years of qualifying service credit, an applied interest rate of 6 percent or less (compounded annually) will be paid on teaching contributions.
- With less than three years of qualifying service credit, an interest rate of 4 percent or less (compounded annually) will be paid on teaching contributions.

Monthly Payments vs. Account Withdrawal		
Plan Feature	**Monthly Payments**	**Account Withdrawal**
Lifetime monthly benefit	Yes	No
Survivor benefits	Yes	No
Access to healthcare coverage	Yes	No
Cost-of-living adjustments	Yes	No
Direct control over funds	No	Yes
Possible rollover to a qualified plan	No	Yes
Possible tax penalties	No	Yes
Death benefits	Yes	No
Possible investment costs	No	Yes
Individual investment risk	No	Yes
Subject to reemployment guidelines for Ohio public positions	Yes	No
Receive at least the member contributions you have made to STRS Ohio	Yes	Yes

Table K

SUMMARY: Chapter 11

- Many decisions at retirement are irreversible, and it's important to consider all factors before making those decisions.
- With a Single Life Pension Annuity, receive maximum monthly benefits for the remainder of your lifetime.
- With a Joint and Survivor Pension Annuity, you will receive a reduced monthly benefit for the duration of your life. Choose one of several options for providing benefits to one or more beneficiaries after your death.
- Life Annuity Certain and Continuous means you will receive monthly benefits, while a beneficiary will also receive benefits for a specified number of years.
- You can designate up to four beneficiaries for a Multiple Beneficiary Annuity.
- Many retirement options require the consent of your spouse.
- Explore life insurance options before making final payout decisions.
- Some plans offer the option to change from one type to another under certain circumstances.

12

BENEFICIARY DECISIONS AND AVOIDING PROBATE COSTS

No one likes thinking about the end of their lives. One of the few things we have control over is deciding who will receive our assets. It's important that your intentions are clear in order to avoid additional family strife and possible costly probate. *Probate* is the legal process by which many assets are passed on to your heirs.

Designating Primary And Secondary Beneficiaries

There are many rules regarding which benefit plans can be payable to beneficiaries, how those plans are paid, and how different degrees of annuity or lump sums affect the remainder of those benefits. Most plans require you to select your beneficiary upon retirement. But if beneficiaries are not properly selected, the succession will be automatic based on state retirement law (see Table L on the following page).

Specifically designating a primary and secondary beneficiary is the preferred way to make sure you have a say in where your assets go upon your passing. You are required to have your spouse's written permission if they are *not* your primary beneficiary. Your beneficiary may be a person, several people, a trust, an estate, or an institution such as a church. If the designated beneficiary becomes disallowed or cancelled by law, legal circumstances may arise.

Retirement Law Automatic Succession
Under current law, automatic succession is as follows: In the event of death prior to retirement:
1. Spouse 2. Children 3. Dependent parent If none of the previously listed is applicable, parents share equally in the member's estate.
After retirement, for any amounts due the benefit recipient at the time of his/her death:
1. Spouse 2. Shared equally by children 3. Shared equally by parents 4. Your estate
For the death benefit only:
1. Spouse 2. Shared equally by children 3. Shared equally by parents 4. The person responsible for burial expenses
If none of the previously listed is applicable, the benefit is paid to your estate.

Table L

Marriage, divorce or dissolution of marriage, legal separation, birth, or the adoption of a child can cause a prior specific designation to become invalid. It is important to always update your beneficiaries to reflect any major life changes.

If you don't send a new designation to your plan administrator after one of these events occurs, the beneficiary will instead be determined either by automatic succession or by the last beneficiary designation. If you take a lump sum for any portion of your account, the beneficiary designation ceases for the portion taken by you.

If you are survived by a child (or children) who is unmarried, under the age of 18 (or age 22 and also a student), they may only receive monthly annuity benefits. Children who are deemed physically or mentally incompetent, regardless of age, also come directly under a spouse in beneficiary determination. If your beneficiary is a trust, an estate, or an institution (as opposed to a person), that beneficiary is not eligible for regular monthly benefits. They will instead receive a lump sum of the current value or portion thereof of your plan.

If you fail to designate a beneficiary for death benefits at retirement, the beneficiary designated on your retirement application will receive a lump sum death benefit upon your passing. Should your designated beneficiary predecease you and you do not designate a replacement beneficiary, a lump sum death benefit will be paid under automatic succession as listed in Table L located on the previous page.

Notice Of Death

You cannot provide notice of your own death, of course. However, it is your responsibility to ensure that those you leave behind know to get in touch with the administrator(s) of your retirement plan(s), as well as those of all other retirement accounts and life insurance policies.

Life Insurance

Death benefits from life insurance policies avoid probate with proper beneficiary designations, so they are generally paid to beneficiaries quickly. Make sure the person handling your affairs is aware of your policy and knows who to contact.

It is worth reiterating that benefits are distributed based on who you have listed as beneficiary. If you have "old" beneficiaries listed, whom you *intended* to replace, they will under most circumstances receive the benefit, regardless of what may make reasonable sense; what matters is what is on file for your account, not your intentions.

Once proof of death is established and the insurance company is sent a copy, the death benefit is paid within days or weeks. Other funds and bank accounts, however, are typically frozen until ownership is clearly established. When choosing a beneficiary, consider whether someone will need to access those funds quickly upon your death. If payments need to be made for end-of-life costs such as burial, mortgage costs, or loan payments, access to these funds may be critical.

For this reason, a minor child may not be the best primary beneficiary. You may want to allocate a specific dollar amount or percentage to someone who can be trusted to cover costs of your burial and other end-of-life obligations for a month or two. If you do name a minor child as beneficiary and then fail to name a guardian, or place the proceeds in a trust for that child, the state may assign someone to manage the money on your child's behalf until they reach age 18.

Wills

A will is a legal document that allows a person to make decisions about how his or her estate will be managed and distributed after their death.

Wills must go through probate. This process can take months or even years. And no assets are distributed until the probate process is complete. This can cause financial hardship for a family when the deceased left property that needs to be maintained. The process of determining the intent behind a will can also destroy familial closeness. A feeling of inequity and unfairness can create hard feelings. If you use a will as an estate planning tool, make sure that the person (or people) receiving property or assets, as specified in that will, is capable of waiting to receive them.

Revocable Living Trust

For those worried that a will can tie up assets for too long, one potential solution is a revocable living trust.[67] While defining the full details of a revocable living trust is outside the scope of this book, it is important for you to know that such a trust exists, and that it allows assets to be held safely by a trustee until they can be distributed directly to beneficiaries in a manner that avoids probate.

In Ohio, you can make a revocable living trust for most assets you own. This includes cars, real estate, collectibles, bank accounts, and anything material and of value. You remain the trustee for the duration of your life, and you name a successor trustee to take charge upon your death. At that point, the successor trustee transfers assets to the trust beneficiaries named in the document, which successfully avoids probate.

There are many other reasons to have a living trust, which may include protecting inherited assets from creditors, specifying ages when your children will have access to money, properly taking care of special needs children, and more.

Non-Pension Retirement Plans

Hopefully, by the point of retirement, you have ample money stashed away. You may have maxed out contributions on your 403(b) or 457(b) plans. You may have IRAs that you've forgotten about. Wherever you may have money stored, it's imperative that a plan is in place for who will inherit any leftovers after you pass away. Be sure these plans are reflected in your beneficiary designations.

A good Financial Quarterback will point out to you that an inherited retirement plan often requires the withdrawal of funds over time. Remember, the money on those accounts is tax deferred, and the IRS wants the taxes they haven't collected yet. Therefore, upon your death, the new owner will be required to start taking distributions so some of that tax revenue can start trickling in. And the older the beneficiary inheriting the account, the shorter their life expectancy will be; higher required distributions will reflect that.

●   ●   ●

The Importance Of Consistency

The beneficiaries named in your pension account, savings vehicles, and life insurance policies should match what is stipulated in your will and estate plan. As an example, if your previous spouse is named as the beneficiary of your 403(b) in the documents on file with the custodian, while your current spouse is named as the beneficiary of that plan in your will, the 403(b) plan designation should supersede the will and your previous spouse would inherit the funds, not your current spouse, even if your will is the more recent document.

Choosing the best beneficiaries for your mix of assets is an intricate process; it's important to think about how these inheritances will affect their taxes, as well as whether they may cause any legal issues. This is another reason why having a Financial Quarterback on your team is so helpful; a strong financial advisor will be able to assist you with building a team of specialists that can answer your questions and help you avoid potential problems like this.

Beware Of Probate

A client once told me, "Probate is the traffic jam that I never want to be stuck in again." This sentiment is familiar with anyone who has been through this process of waiting and uncertainty after the death of a loved one.

Probate: Is the legal process by which many assets are passed on to your heirs. The probate period includes a public notice of death, which allows creditors to file claims against the estate. After any creditor claims are settled, the estate is distributed in accordance with the will. In cases where there is no will, the state will decide how to distribute your property. Probate proceedings are public; sometimes certain circumstances may mean the public nature of probate creates additional problems for the heirs, so it's all the more important to do what you can ahead of time to minimize the impact.

Work with your Financial Quarterback to set up your affairs so that as many of your assets as possible will avoid probate altogether. This way, there's less likelihood the court will need to make decisions on your behalf, and property won't be tied up for up to a year or longer. As a rule, less time spent in probate means lower legal costs, which are usually paid for out of the estate.

Simplified Probate Procedures For Small Estates

The state of Ohio has a simplified probate process for small estates. Covered under Ohio Revised Code Ann. § 2113.03,[68] anyone who has a small estate themselves, or who is helping a friend or family member with a small estate find solutions, should be aware of it. You may implement this code, distribute assets, and avoid most or all of the hassles of regular probate if the following conditions exist:

1. The value of the estate is $35,000 or less.
2. The surviving spouse inherits everything, either under a will or by law, and value of the estate is $100,000 or less.

Small estates can easily be eaten up by legal costs; this particular section of code has saved a good deal of time and money for many people who need a quick settlement.

Selecting An Executor

An *executor* is the person with the legal responsibility to ensure that all of the deceased's wishes for their estate are carried out. It is the executor's role to make sure taxes get paid, bills and debts are satisfied, and assets are transferred properly.

When selecting someone to fulfill these responsibilities, look for a person who is trustworthy and will be partial to your wishes. Choose someone who has an understanding of the rules and who can recognize (and admit) where they may need guidance from someone with more experience. If you don't appoint an executor, the court will appoint one for you, and it's hard to imagine that the court's judgment would be better than yours in such an important decision. You're asking a lot of this individual; pick someone who is up to the task and can get the job done. As time goes by, you are always free to change who is named executor. Remember, this job isn't a reward; it is, in fact, a favor.

If no one you know has the necessary qualifications, consider naming a professional—hiring someone who is not in the family or part of a circle of friends who can create peace of mind while minimizing family disputes. Whoever you appoint, be it a family member or a professional, be sure to take into consideration their geographical location; you want someone who lives near you.

Now Is The Time

Don't wait to get all your affairs in order. Now is the best time to name beneficiaries, revisit guidelines regarding your spouse, peruse court orders, and otherwise know all the rules so that you can be sure your retirement accounts, insurance policies, and other documents are in order. The fewer items that can be contested, the easier and cheaper it will be for those you leave behind.

Keeping items out of probate will reduce costs for those left behind and free up those assets for use sooner. Be sure to speak with your Financial Quarterback about all your options to see which decisions might be best for you. These are never anyone's favorite things to think about, but there is a certain comfort that comes when you know everything is taken care of and nothing has been left undone.

SUMMARY: Chapter 12

- Always keep primary and secondary beneficiaries up to date.
- Appoint a trusted individual with the task of making all legal notifications of your death.
- Wills don't avoid probate. Nevertheless, they are a popular estate-planning tool.
- Make a plan for who will inherit all of your other, non-pension accounts when you pass away.
- Make certain that those named to inherit various accounts and assets in your will are consistent with named beneficiaries for each account.
- Probate is a time-consuming, sometimes costly process through which assets are passed on to heirs. Know the laws and do what you can to avoid probate when prudent.
- Selecting the right executor for your estate is important. Make sure taxes and bills get paid and that all your property goes where you wish. If you don't choose, the court will choose for you.

SECTION 3

OHIO EMPLOYEE RETIREMENT PLAN DIFFERENCES

13

OPERS: OHIO PUBLIC EMPLOYEE RETIREMENT SYSTEM

The Ohio Public Employee Retirement System (OPERS) provides retirement, disability, and survivor benefit programs for public employees throughout the state of Ohio who are not otherwise covered by another state or local retirement system. OPERS serves more than 1 million past and present Ohio workers and had over $94.1 billion in net assets as of the end of 2018. OPERS is the largest pension fund in Ohio and the 12th largest public retirement system in the country.

There is serious and frequent discussion among state legislators focused on reducing the retirement benefits that members of OPERS have spent their working lives accumulating. While no one individual may be able to halt the long-term momentum of public sentiment, you can, to some extent, protect yourself by making sure you and your family have coordinated and managed your future entitlements before you retire.

For an OPERS member to effectively manage their retirement, they need the knowledge to make informed personal decisions and the initiative to take action now. The goal should be to maximize the individual benefits available under your personal pension and any deferred compensation plans, and to consider whether a Partial Lump Sum Option Payment (PLOP)[69] may be right for you.

Look at all the other factors affecting your retirement—Social Security benefits, other savings plans, potential medical costs, spousal retirement plans, changes in the cost of living, and other factors discussed in earlier chapters. Build your team and find the right Financial Quarterback to get all the players working together and you will go much further.

First, a word about groups, for the Traditional and the Combined Plan, your eligibility, and, ultimately, your benefits depend on which group you fall into—either A, B, or C. Your group can be found either on your latest OPERS statement or by registering and logging into your account online. The Member-Directed Plan, outlined below, does not make use of these groups.

Traditional Pension Plan

For the Defined Benefit Plan, or "Traditional Pension Plan" as it's more commonly known, your eventual benefit will be determined by one of two formulas. Remember the part about finding out what group you're in? Whether you're in Group A, B, or C determines when you're eligible to retire and how your retirement benefit will be calculated. Your group also affects when you will be eligible for healthcare coverage through OPERS.

Groups A & B

For members in Groups A and B, the retirement benefit consists of an annual lifetime allowance equal to 2.2 percent of your final average salary, multiplied by the first 30 years of service plus 2.5 percent of final average salary for each year, or partial year for service credit over 30.

The Formula:
2.2% of Final Average Service x Years of Service
(For the First 30 years) Plus (+)
2.5% of Final Average Service (For each year over 30).

Group C

For members in Group C, the retirement benefit consists of an annual lifetime allowance equal to 2.2 percent of your final average salary, multiplied by the first 35 years of service plus 2.5 percent of final average salary for each year, or partial year for service credit over 35.

The Formula:
2.2% of Final Average Service x Years of Service
(For the First 35 years) Plus (+)
2.5% of Final Average Service (For each year over 35).

Disability Benefits

OPERS has two disability programs, the Original Plan and the Revised Plan. Enrollment is based solely on when you became an OPERS member. Members hired prior to July 29, 1992, are in the Original Plan, unless the member chose coverage under the Revised Plan. Members hired after July 29, 1992, are only covered by the Revised Plan.

Survivor Benefits

Your loved ones may qualify to receive survivor benefits if you should pass away before you retire or while you're receiving a disability benefit. In order to qualify for these benefits, you must have at least 18 months of full-time service at the time of death.

It's important to designate a beneficiary (or beneficiaries), and to keep this information up-to-date. Depending on who you designate as your beneficiary, your survivors will receive either a monthly benefit or a lump sum.

Healthcare

Although not a guaranteed benefit, as of 2019, OPERS offers healthcare coverage to retirees age 60 or older with at least 20 years of qualifying service and to all retirees with 30 to 32 years of qualifying service, and depending on the retirement group they fit into. To determine if and when you may qualify, check with your benefits counselor, or consult the Pension and Healthcare Eligibility Guide online.[70]

Combined Pension Plan

The Combined Plan is a hybrid plan that includes both a defined benefit and defined contribution component. Your eventual benefit is calculated from the total of both portions. The contributions from yours will be managed by OPERS and their investment professionals, while your member contributions will be managed in a way that you choose from the available OPERS investment options. This is similar to the way a 401(k) plan might work at a private company or organization.

As with the Traditional Plan, the defined benefit portion of the calculation will be determined by your group (A, B, or C). And, these formulas take into consideration your retirement group, your years of service, and your final average salary. The explanation of the formulas, taken directly from the OPERS website, are as follows:

Groups A & B

For members in Groups A and B, the retirement benefit calculated under the Combined Plan consists of an annual lifetime allowance equal to 2.2 percent of the final average salary, multiplied by the first 30 years of service plus 2.5 percent of final average salary for each year, or partial year for service credit over 30.

Formula:
1% of Final Average Service x Years of Service
(For the First 30 Years) Plus (+)
1.25% Final Average Service (For each year over 30).

Group C

For members in Group C, the retirement benefit calculated under the Combined Plan consists of an annual lifetime allowance equal to 2.2 percent of the final average salary, multiplied by the first 35 years of service plus 2.5 percent of final average salary for each year, or partial year for service credit over 35.

Formula:
1% of Final Average Service x Years of Service
(For the First 35 Years) Plus (+)
1.25% Final Average Service (For each year over 35).

Unlike with the Traditional Plan, the defined contribution benefit you will receive, if you choose to annuitize, is based on the amount you contributed. It is affected by expenses, account gains and losses in the OPERS investment options you select, and also annuity aspects, like your retirement age.

Disability Benefits

Disability benefits are offered through one of OPERS' two plans, as defined above in the Traditional Plan.

Survivor Benefits

Survivor benefits are offered through the defined benefit portion of the plan, and are the same as those offered under the Traditional Plan.

Healthcare

Although not a guaranteed benefit, as of 2019, OPERS offers the same healthcare options available as part of the Traditional Pension Plan.

Member-Directed Plan

The Member-Directed Plan is a defined contribution plan, which allows you to direct how your contributions are invested. Consequently, under this plan, you bear sole responsibility for any investment risks.

Your benefit will be based on the amount you contributed over the course of your career. It is also affected by expenses, account gains and losses, and various annuity factors such as your retirement age. The calculation formula for members in the member-directed plan who choose to take a monthly benefit is their final account value, multiplied by an annuity factor.

Final Account Value:
(Employee and Employer Contributions, with any investment gains/
    *losses) x Annuity Factor **
*(OPERS actuaries determine annuity factors by applying
    underlying interest rate and mortality assumptions to a standard
    annuity formula).

Disability Benefits

Disability benefits are not offered through the Member-Directed Plan. However, you do have the option (under certain circumstances) to change plans from Member-Directed to either the Traditional or the Combined Plan. If you decide to switch, at least one year must pass from the effective date of your plan change before you can apply for disability benefits in your new plan.

Survivor Benefits

Unlike the Traditional and Combined Plans, the Member-Directed Plan does not provide survivor benefits. However, upon your death, the vested portion of your individual account balance will be paid to your beneficiaries in a onetime lump sum payment.

Healthcare

Under the Member-Directed Plan, a percentage of employer contributions will be credited to a retiree medical account, which will be managed by an outside vendor. Unlike your individual account, OPERS administrates and directs the investment of this account. This account may be used for the payment of qualified healthcare expenses such as insurance premiums, deductibles, medical copays, and services, and may even be used toward transportation to receive medical care. It can also include limited amounts paid for any qualified long-term-care insurance.

Managing Health Insurance Costs

When you retire, if you are eligible, you and your dependents will have the option to participate in the OPERS-sponsored healthcare plan. This plan includes prescription drug coverage, dental, and a vision plan. The premiums would be deducted from your monthly benefit check.

There have been big changes to this plan in the past decade in an effort to keep it solvent. For those who qualify, the pension provides a set allowance each month for healthcare costs based on your total length of service. As you consider this, it is important that you weigh the premium costs; if your spouse is not retiring just yet, it may make sense for you to become a part of *their* plan instead, and then reevaluate when they do retire. You may enroll in the OPERS-sponsored health plan within 31 days of your coverage being canceled by another group plan. You may also reenroll during the regular open enrollment period (contact your plan administrator for details, as the dates change from year to year).

To be eligible for the coverage, you must be age 60 or older with 20 or more years of service. You may also be eligible if you are younger but have 30 to 32 years of service. The variations depend on any rule changes that may have taken place during your employment.

If you are eligible, OPERS healthcare plans also allow you to enroll eligible family members. This includes a legal spouse (you will be required to provide a valid marriage certificate) and children. Eligible children (under age 26; older children who are permanently disabled may also be eligible) must be biological or legally adopted. In some cases, a grandchild is also eligible if they are born to your minor child and the courts have required your job to provide coverage.

Those below certain income limits may be eligible for a discount program, which reduces the cost of your healthcare premiums from OPERS. This is intended to help pay medical and pharmacy premiums for qualified non-Medicare participants. Enrollment for this program occurs during the normal open enrollment period, or within 60 days of first receiving benefits.

OPERS – For Qualified Non-Medicare Participants

Single Person	$23,500
Single With One Dependent	$31,860
Single With Two Or More Dependents	$40,180
Married	$31,860
Married With One Or More Dependents	$40,180

Table M

A dental plan is available as an additional option. Premiums for this are 100 percent the participant's responsibility. OPERS also offers two optional vision plans. For up-to-date info regarding these options, consult your plan's administrator.

Purchasing Service Credits

Service credit is one of the things taken into consideration when determining retirement eligibility and the total retirement benefit amount, as it applies to both the Traditional and Combined Plans. Total service credit under these plans is the length of time you have contributed service and earned "time," as well as additional time purchased through the system as service credits in order to reduce the length of time until retirement eligibility.

Within OPERS, there is also the option to purchase credit for other types of service, including out-of-state federal service, military service, leaves of absence, and services that were otherwise exempt. Purchasing service credits like this is done using a form obtained from OPERS.

In which plan is the service credit earned?

Under the defined benefit plan, calculation of eligibility and amount of a retirement payout is used to determine the full amount of the combined plan. There are specific requirements, including the achievement of necessary years for age and service benefits. The amount of total service credit you have is used to determine your retirement benefits.

A Member-Directed Plan does not have these requirements. Your contributions, any employer-matched contributions, and the performance of the underlying assets determine how much you will benefit.

OPERS allows you to enhance your overall retirement payments by using pre-tax dollars to buy additional service credits (see Chapter 9 for more information). Under most situations, it is advisable to take advantage of as many opportunities to do this as possible.

In most cases, overtime pay will count toward service credits. Accumulated sick leave, on the other hand, does not count toward the defined benefit calculation. Part of the retirement planning process under OPERS is to properly coordinate all these inputs, including coordinating vacation, sick pay, and the deferred compensation payout.

Partial Lump Sum Option Plan (PLOP)

Participants in OPERS also have the option of a Partial Lump Sum Option Plan (PLOP). This type of plan allows retiring pension plan participants to receive a lump sum up front, which comes out of your overall pension; recipients still receive monthly benefits, but those payments are reduced.

The amount of the lump sum is determined by the employee, but it cannot be less than 6 times or more than 36 times the amount that would be collected under traditional pension payments. The sum requested must be in denominations of $1,000, unless either the minimum or maximum amount is selected. To put it more simply, you may take up to three years' worth of payment in one check at retirement (or roll that money over to a self-directed IRA), but no less than a month and a half's worth. The amount taken will reduce your monthly payment going forward according to a complex formula.

One of the main reasons you might opt for a PLOP is if you don't *need* all the monthly income derived by the traditional pension payout to support the lifestyle you want in retirement. Maybe your spouse has a very strong pension so you will not need all of yours, or perhaps you have been very disciplined and saved a lot of money in your other retirement accounts that will provide more than enough supplemental income. There are many scenarios that make this PLOP attractive, making it necessary to sit down with a professional who can help you make the right decision.

For most people, once you and your spouse have passed away, the pension also stops; their children would not receive any additional inheritance from it. However, taking a PLOP enables you to roll over some of that money to a self-directed IRA. With proper management, any remaining money in that account will go directly to your beneficiaries, instead of being lost to the pension.

SUMMARY: Chapter 13

- Make sure you fully understand the differences between the Defined Benefit, the Combined, and the Self-Directed Plans, as well as which group you're included in.
- OPERS-sponsored healthcare and related options are a significant benefit in retirement. Find out what you qualify for and enroll within the appropriate time frame.
- Determine if you are eligible to purchase service credits, and if the benefit to doing so would outweigh the cost.
- Decide if a Partial Lump Sum Option Plan fits your financial needs and goals.
- Discuss your situation with your Financial Quarterback and others such as a tax attorney to help ensure you are meeting your retirement needs and protecting your estate/loved ones when you are gone.

14

STRS:
STATE TEACHERS
RETIREMENT SYSTEM

As the father of three school-aged children, I am more than aware of the importance of having the very best teachers mentoring our youth to academic excellence. I also know from experience that teachers often spend more time focused on their students' growth than on their own financial future.

This occupational hazard is made worse by the fact that states' budget constraints are forcing communities throughout the country to work toward permanently reducing the earned pension benefits teachers have spent their entire careers earning. Proactive measures were discussed in Section 1, and the importance of these steps is increasing each year. It has always been incumbent on you to coordinate and manage your own future entitlements and to do it while you're still working.

Teachers selflessly spend their days preparing young minds for the future, often to the detriment of their own futures. There is no better time than the present to secure that future.

Educators are covered by the State Teachers Retirement System (STRS),[71] which is similar to OPERS in that it also offers Defined Benefit, Defined Contribution, and Combined Plans. However, some members may have the option of an Alternative Retirement Plan (ARP).[72] These are generally administered by a third-party vendor, and can vary dramatically. Generally speaking, if these are available to you, it's best to contact the third-party vendor about the details of these plans. However, all of the plans share some commonalities, which we'll discuss below.

Defined Benefit Plan

Under the Defined Benefit (DB) Plan,[73] your retirement income will be calculated using your total years of service, your average salary during that service, and your age. Members will receive 2.2 percent of their five-year final average salary for each year of service. Members can receive a benefit at age 65, provided they have 5 years of service, or at any age, provided they have 32 years of service.

However, there are eligibility guidelines for unreduced benefits at any age that have recently increased. As of March of 2019, these are:

- 33 years of credit required: beginning August 1, 2019
- 34 years of credit required: beginning August 1, 2021
- 35 years of credit required: August 1, 2023–July 1, 2026

Starting August 1, 2026, beneficiaries must be age 60 with 35 years of service, or age 65 with 5 years of service, in order to receive an unreduced benefit.

Members can retire early with actuarially reduced benefits at age 60 if they have five years of service; the same applies for someone who is age 55 with 27 years of service. However, the service credit requirement for early retirement at age 55 will be increasing:

- 28 years' service required: beginning August 1, 2019
- 29 years' service required: August 1, 2021–July 1, 2023

All members with at least 30 years of service are eligible for early retirement with a reduced benefit, no matter what their age.

In all of these scenarios, under Defined Benefits, members are able to combine credits from other Ohio public pension plans.

Disability Benefits

If a member becomes disabled while employed and has at least 10 years of service, they are able to apply for disability benefits, and that application window remains open for up to one year following their last date of STRS-covered service. Members will receive 2.2 percent of final salary per year of service, between 45–60 percent of final average salary, and, at age 65, the member will convert to service retirement and will also receive credit for the period of disability.

Survivor Benefits

Members are eligible for survivor benefits with five years of service credit. Qualified survivors will receive the highest among three options below for which they are eligible.

Retirement Based: If the member had met the age and service requirements for retirement, then the survivor will be able receive a benefit in the same manner as if the member had actually retired and selected a same-to-beneficiary Joint and Survivor Annuity. If there are no minor children, a lump sum withdrawal is also an option.

Dependent Based: From 25 percent to 60 percent of final average salary based on the number of eligible survivors.

Service Based: From 29 percent of final average salary with 20 years of service credit, and up to 60 percent of final average salary with 29 years of service based on the years of credit the member had at the time of death.

Healthcare

Anyone receiving benefits (including disability or survivor benefits) and their dependents may be eligible for access to healthcare coverage. Coverage can include hospitalization, physician fees, and prescriptions. Dental and vision coverage are also available to some members. Eligibility is based on certain requirements; see your plan administrator for up-to-date information (also covered in more depth later in this chapter).

Combined Plan

Under the Combined Plan, retirement income is based on separate retirement benefits that are paid from the defined benefit and defined contribution portions of the member's STRS account. Income from the defined contribution part is based on the value of the member's account at retirement. Members are eligible to take regular monthly payments in the form of a lifetime annuity from this balance at age 50. The annuity is calculated by dividing the account balance by an annuity factor, and the annuity rates are based on market conditions and subject to change. Members are eligible to begin receiving benefits at age 60 with five years of service. The annual defined benefit amount is 1 percent of a five-year final average salary per year of service. The Combined Plan is not eligible for a combined retirement benefit with other Ohio public pension plans.

Disability Benefits

Members are eligible to receive disability if they have 10 years of service credit. Both the employer's and member's contributions, in addition to any investment gains in the defined contribution account, will be used to fund the benefit. Members will receive 2.2 percent of their final average salary per year of experience along with between 45–60 percent of their final average salary. At age 65, the member will convert to service retirement and receive credit for the period of disability. The account balance is also available to the member.

Healthcare

STRS is clear that, like with OPERs, healthcare coverage is not guaranteed, and STRS may change or discontinue any or all of its healthcare benefits in the future. Currently, however, members receiving disability benefits and family members receiving survivor benefits have access to the healthcare coverage provided under the Defined Benefit Plan, provided they meet certain requirements (covered in more depth later in this chapter).

Likewise, members under the Combined Plan who opt for monthly retirement benefits at age 60 and who meet eligibility requirements will also have access to healthcare coverage. Dental and vision coverage may also be available.

Defined Contribution (DC) Plan

In this plan, benefits received are based on the amount in the account, both member and employer contributions, as well as the performance of investment decisions and the effective annuity rate at the time of retirement. Members are able to take a lifetime annuity in retirement starting at age 50. This annuity is calculated by dividing the account balance by an annuity factor, which is based on effective market rates at the time of the retirement. The DC Plan cannot be combined with other Ohio pension plans. Members are vested in their own contributions immediately, and become vested in employer contributions at a rate of 20 percent per year.

Disability Benefits

The account balance of the plan is available to members who terminate and withdraw their account. At age 50, other payment options are available, but employment must first be terminated.

Survivor Benefits

Under Defined Contributions, survivor benefits are available to beneficiaries in the form of the remaining account balance.

Healthcare

Healthcare coverage is not available under Defined Contributions.

Alternative Retirement Plans (ARPs)

Some organizations may offer Alternative Retirement Plans to employees. These are administered by third-party vendors, who are generally the best source of information on these plans. However, all plans share the same contributions, which are currently 14 percent from the participant and 9.53 percent from the employer.

Disability Benefits

Participants who terminate employment and withdraw their account will have access to disability benefits from their remaining account balance.

Survivor Benefits

The account balance will be made available to beneficiaries.

Healthcare

Healthcare coverage is not included.

A Good Start

Everyone's situation is unique. While this chapter is intended to help provide a basic overview of retirement options for STRS members, don't let this book be your only source of information. You can and should learn more by speaking with your benefits counselor and by consulting the STRS website, which has been an invaluable resource in compiling this chapter. You can find more information, along with helpful charts, flyers, leaflets, and other documents, at the STRS website.

Prepare For Big Changes In Retirement Benefits

Once, Ohio teachers could assume that their retirement benefits were unlikely to decrease before retirement. After official retirement, those benefits were safe and would be "grandfathered" into any future changes.

However, it is no longer safe to assume that. Years of operating in challenging economic times has recently caused the STRS of Ohio to set in motion cost-cutting measures that will have a direct impact on your retirement benefits. This makes it more important than ever for you to plan as early as possible. In fact, on September 26, 2012, Governor John Kasich signed pension reform bills into law, which enacted changes that the STRS Board had been working on since 2009.

Many of these changes will affect your retirement and pension. These include an expectation for increasingly larger employee contributions, decisions to retire at higher ages, and the effect of years of service on monthly benefits. Also, a reduction of cost-of-living adjustments (COLAs) will have a negative effect, as will reductions that decrease the benefit formula for your pension and a host of other, lesser reductions.

Teachers should take to heart the same advice given to anyone preparing to retire: before deciding when, take the time to find out how much money you will need monthly after taxes and insurance to enjoy a comfortable retirement. Obviously, the changes mentioned above can have a significant impact on your future, and your goal should be to minimize the negative impact of these changes.

To do this, consider securing the help of a qualified independent financial advisor, a Financial Quarterback, to work with you on a thorough plan tailored to your specific situation. Financial professionals specializing in government employees will know the intricacies and options that go into creating a coordinated plan for your specific situation. Ultimately, a good financial team pays for itself.

Reducing Taxes Pre-Retirement

If you are over age 50, the first thing you should do is to make sure you are utilizing the catch-up provisions discussed in Chapter 7.

Budget cuts have dampened the rise in teacher salaries and also in employer contributions to STRS pension plans. Take the lead yourself and put as much as is allowed into separate 403(b) or 457(b) retirement accounts, both as regular contributions and as catch-ups. Doing this can help you make up for any potential retirement shortfalls and these contributions are generally all pre-tax and grow tax deferred.

You should also be aware of (and take advantage of) the traditional IRA and Roth IRA contributions that make the most sense for your particular tax, family, and legacy situation. In addition to being used as retirement funds, Roth IRAs can also be a great way to accumulate money for a child's education while also providing them the best opportunity to qualify for financial aid.

Using PLOP Effectively

Opting for a Partial Lump Sum Option Payment (PLOP) will lower your monthly pension payments after you retire. The up-front benefit of PLOP, of course, is that it allows you to take a lump sum distribution at retirement and perhaps put it into a self-directed IRA, where you can receive additional returns. If you follow the IRS rules, you will not trigger any penalties while rolling over this "qualified" money. STRS and your Financial Quarterback can give you a breakdown of your pension payment options with different scenarios.

If you roll the lump sum into an IRA, you may be able to invest it in a way that grows more than it would have otherwise, given the STRS's cost of living adjustments. In 2017, STRS froze cost-of-living adjustments for five years, meaning there is no COLA until 2022. "If they do not restore the COLA before 2022, the average teacher in Ohio and the average *retired* teacher, will lose $12,000 a year every year for the rest of their life, even if they restore the COLA," according to retiree Bob Buerkle.[74]

Unlike pension funds, which revert back to the state when you and your spouse pass, an IRA can legally allow your PLOP funds to pass directly to your designated beneficiaries. This is a big deal; nothing taken as a lump sum this way goes back to the state. It instead becomes part of your legacy.

Purchasing Service Credits

Another thing to consider as you approach retirement is service credits. If you can purchase them, consider buying as many as you can. Total service credit under these plans is the length of time you have actually contributed service and earned as "time" *or* any amount you have purchased into the system to reduce the time for retirement eligibility. Determining eligibility and purchasing service is done through a form you can obtain from STRS. You may use pre-tax earnings to buy additional service credits. In most cases, overtime pay will also be used as part of the retirement benefit calculation. Part of the planning process under STRS is to properly coordinate all these inputs; vacation, sick pay, and deferred compensation payout must all be taken into account.

Reversion

Another nuance specific to teachers is the reversion option. If a teacher originally selects the Joint and Survivor option but is willing to take a slightly lower pension payment, and their (non-teacher) spouse passes away first, the teacher then has the right to switch to the higher payout, sole survivor option. However, the "with reversion" option must be selected on the date of pension election for this to be available.

Maximizing Social Security Benefits

It's important to plan for the Social Security Windfall Elimination Provision (WEP). If you have 30 or more years of "substantial" earnings with an employer where you paid Social Security taxes, you might be able to eliminate the offset by as much as 67 percent of your Social Security benefits, up to the current maximum offset of $480 in 2020. Every year has to be accounted for, and you must follow the Social Security tables. You're Financial Quarterback or any good financial planning office will have these tables and keep them up-to-date; you should check and see if you qualify. (WEP was covered in depth in Chapter 10).

You should also plan around and for the Government Pension Offset (GPO). If you receive a pension from a federal, state, or local government based on work where you did not pay Social Security taxes, but you are also eligible for Social Security from another source (other employment), your spouse's, widow's, or widower's Social Security benefits may be reduced as a result. (GPO was also covered in Chapter 10).

Healthcare

Ohio state law does not guarantee healthcare coverage for public school employees, but STRS has continued to provide for medical care and prescription drug costs anyway, as they are an important part of a financially sound retirement. Cuts in school district budgets have made healthcare options less favorable to spouses and children, however, so it may be worth periodically evaluating alternate coverage options for your loved ones.

STRS offers healthcare to its benefit participants after they have achieved 15 or more years of qualifying service. Educators retiring after August 1, 2023, cannot enroll until they have 20 or more years of service.

If you are a STRS participant choosing to retire before age 65, when you might otherwise qualify for Medicare, you may qualify for STRS health benefits if you have at least 15 years of service. If this stipulation applies to you, STRS will subsidize your individual monthly healthcare premium at the 2012 rate of 2.4 percent for each year of service credit, up to a maximum of 72 percent.

This subsidy has been changing; like so many other benefits, it has become less generous in recent years. Beginning in 2013 and continuing through 2015, the subsidy rate for healthcare decreased by 0.1 percent per year. As of 2015, the level of subsidy was 2.1 percent and capped out at a maximum 63 percent of healthcare premiums. Spouses and dependent children of qualified retirees (those with 15 or more years of service) are eligible to join the STRS healthcare plan as well, but they are charged full premiums.

All of these costs may seem small, but they accumulate and can be a drain on your retirement income.

Preserve And Protect Retirement Assets

Review the tax strategies discussed throughout Section 2; they aren't just for the affluent. These strategies will allow you to increase the funds available to you in retirement, further improve your monthly cash flow by cost reduction, and protect your assets from litigation and catastrophic illness.

Many former teachers want to stay busy during their retirement years. Consider capitalizing on your years of professional experience with a new line of work maybe tutoring, substitute teaching, or a shift to the private sector, among other options. If you do any type of consulting or start your own business, you might be able to deduct up to 100 percent of your healthcare premiums. Please speak with your Financial Quarterback about making these strategies work for you.

●   ●   ●

SUMMARY: Chapter 14

- Your pension benefits may be reduced in the future. Rising retirement ages, higher years of service determinants, and higher personal contributions are not out of the question.
- Make catch-up provisions as soon as you're eligible, to reduce your current tax bill.
- Using PLOP effectively may give you more options in retirement.
- Determine your service credit eligibility and purchase as much as you can.
- The reversion option allows you to change from Joint and Survivor to Single Life. Consider carefully whether this is a good idea for your situation.
- Know how the WEP and GPO may affect your Social Security benefits.
- STRS offers healthcare coverage to qualifying participants and their families.
- Utilize every tax strategy available to you to keep your finances working efficiently throughout retirement.
- Discuss your situation with your Financial Quarterback and others such as a tax attorney to help ensure you are meeting your retirement needs and protecting your estate/loved ones when you are gone.

15

OP&F:
OHIO POLICE AND FIRE

A s a former police officer, I understand what it's like to be in the trenches. You're having a nice, calm day one minute; the next, you're off to a call with lights and sirens blaring, adrenaline pumping, and senses on high alert.

Plan For The Unexpected

Emergency workers are surely a group of professionals who deserves the ability to step aside and enjoy the pension and benefits due to them as part of an agreement made many years earlier, after working years full of sacrifice and risk.

However, the compensation these public service workers were promised is facing pressure from many directions. Firefighters and police officers facing the end of their careers have spent decades working hard and deserve to enjoy the compensation they're due upon retirement. It's important for these men and women to take steps on their own to maximize what they have; firefighters and police officers, of all people, understand that being prepared for the unexpected can avert disaster.

If you're currently at the end of your career as an emergency worker, you can expect to receive most benefits in retirement as promised. That's why many of the previous chapters were filled with specific retirement planning techniques and pitfalls to avoid.

But as we all know, there are no ironclad guarantees in life. It is fortunate that any new cutbacks are likely to be geared toward those with the most lead time to adjust; those expecting to retire soon will be less affected than those who still have years or decades of work to look forward to. The majority of this chapter summarizes potential pension changes and how you can adapt your plans to compensate, right now.

However, this chapter isn't just for those in mid-career. I've designed this chapter so that many of the tips will prove equally valuable to those near the end of their public service careers.

Remain Aware Of Changes In Retirement Benefits

Some of the changes that will affect younger employees in the OP&F system may include the following:

1. Increased employee contributions.
2. Increased necessary retirement age and years of service to calculate monthly benefits.
3. Reduced cost-of-living adjustments (COLAs).
4. Decreases in the overall benefit formula for your pension.

The bottom line: take the time NOW to determine how much money you will need every month (after taxes and insurance) to enjoy retirement. Any of the changes mentioned above, if they end up affecting you, can have a significant impact on your retirement. Your goal should be to minimize the negative effects of these changes. To do this, consider implementing strategies discussed earlier in this book. They were designed to help you and your money, under most circumstances, to go further than you had planned.

We would also urge you to structure an additional retirement plan outside of that provided by your employer. That way, if one plan fails or otherwise falls short, you know you won't get caught in a difficult situation. The following nine planning strategies will help you do just that.

Maximize Eligible Contributions

If you're over age 50, making all catch-up contributions allowable annually is one way of providing for expenditures big and small in retirement. You're going to live another 25 to 40 years, after all; it's likely you will have a few more new cars and big vacations in your lifetime. Putting money away now in tax deferred savings accounts won't cost you as much in the long-term, and the money will compound, tax deferred.

It is important to understand how to put more money aside into 457(b) retirement accounts to make up for any potential retirement shortfalls. Your 457(b) account does offer the ability to make an extra payment under certain circumstances (see Chapter 6 for more details). These contributions can be pre-tax, and they grow tax deferred.

You should also be aware of and take advantage of the traditional IRA and Roth IRA contributions that make the most sense for your particular tax, family, and legacy situation. While not technically part of your pension benefits, maximizing the amounts of any IRA accounts you hold is a smart idea; the money will be welcome further down the road for unplanned expenses.

Take Full Advantage Of DROP

The Deferred Retirement Option Plan (DROP) can be very beneficial for those who are eligible. Make sure you take advantage of every possible provision.

DROP is an option that allows eligible pension participants to accumulate a tax deferred amount of money during their working years that will ultimately be delivered as a lump sum upon retirement. There is no specific time when you need to take all the money out, but remember that this money is not an annuity to be paid out over the course of your retirement like your regular monthly pension. There are very specific criteria you have to meet to become eligible for DROP, and for those who are eligible, it almost always makes sense to take full advantage.

If your employer has adopted this plan, you become eligible after you have worked and meet the requirements for retirement but then opt to continue working. Rather than have the additional time credited to the benefits formula for your defined pension plan, it goes into a separate (DROP) account. Also added to this account over time is the part of your pay that otherwise would have been used to fund your pension (along with any accumulated interest earnings). This account then becomes eligible for a lump sum distribution at retirement. This lump sum is in addition to your monthly pension.

One thing to consider before entering DROP is whether there is a promotion with a significant pay increase in your future. When you enroll in DROP, your pension is frozen at its current level. If you receive a pay increase after enrolling, your pension will not go up accordingly; your only future increases will come as a result of COLA, not because of your job title or rank.

OP&F uses a variable interest rate for both DROP and reemployed retiree accounts. That interest rate is tied to the 10-year Treasury note; through June 30, 2019, it was set at 2.41 percent. As you can see in Table N, quarterly rates have changed quite a bit. In October 2019 the Ohio Police and Fire Board of Trustees approved a minimum rate of 2.5%. Therefore the first quarter of 2020 was set to 2.5%.[75]

2019 DROP Interest Rates	
Quarter	Interest Rate
1st	2.69%
2nd	2.41%
3rd	2.00%
4th	1.68%
2018 DROP Interest Rates	
Quarter	Interest Rate
1st	2.40%
2nd	2.74%
3rd	2.85%
4th	3.05%

Table N

Once you officially retire, the money in your DROP account can be left where it is, earning a variable interest rate, or it can be rolled over into a traditional IRA. Keep in mind that any money withdrawn prior to age 59 1/2 from DROP does NOT have the 10 percent early distribution penalty as an IRA does. Therefore, you might want to consider keeping enough money in DROP or a 457 account to get you through age 59 1/2. Remember also that withdrawals from a 457 or IRA are still subject to federal and state income taxes.

IRAs can have some benefits over a DROP account because they not only allow more investment options, but might result in you receiving more money overall. IRA withdrawals are not subject to the mandatory 20 percent federal tax withholding that DROP is subject to.

If your tax bracket in retirement is lower than 20 percent, you can choose to have withheld just what is needed for taxes; if your tax rate is 13 percent, you can withhold just 13 percent with a traditional IRA and keep the other 7 percent that would have been withheld in the account, earning money. Under DROP, the government would hold onto this money until you file your taxes each year, forcing you to wait for a refund.

Expand Your Investment Options

Everybody has different needs, and it's important that your retirement plan has a little wiggle room to accommodate any "what-ifs." A police officer may have a special-needs child at home they will care for in perpetuity; a firefighter may be planning to open a small business in their golden years. When it comes to selecting the features and benefits of your 457(b) plans, consideration should be made for your specific needs and situation. You are the one who will have to live with your selections, so it is vital that you pick the plan that will be the best fit. These retirement accounts contain multiple types of investments, so it is also incumbent on you to be vigilant in your regular monitoring of your account, and that you make adjustments if and when market conditions change. An investment or allocation that is expected to do well today may not have the same potential tomorrow.

The average person doesn't realistically have the time or desire to gain a thorough understanding of all of the different types of retirement plans, so it is more important than ever to seek the help of a Financial Quarterback who can not only guide you through the complexity of the choices permitted, but also monitor your accounts appropriately and on an ongoing basis.

A qualified financial advisor, a Registered Investment Advisor (RIA)[76] who helps you set up a 403(b) or 457(b) plan, can take on this burden for you and should be able to actively manage these retirement accounts. RIAs also carry an added layer of fiduciary protection to make sure they are looking out for your best interest, not theirs. See the section, "How To Identify A Financial Quarterback" in Chapter 20 for more information.

Eliminate Spousal Pension Shortfalls

Complete a thorough analysis of joint survivor payout options. One common mistake people make in their calculations is that they believe there are only two pension payout options available—life only and joint survivor. In fact, there are several survivorship options to choose from, including 100 percent, 75 percent, 50 percent, and more.

If you want to make allowances for your spouse, for example, a 50 percent joint survivor option will reduce your lifetime pension payout about 10 percent (depending on age and length of service) in order to provide benefits the remainder of your spouse's lifetime after you die. If you are otherwise eligible to receive $60,000 per annum in life only, opting for a 50 percent joint survivor option will mean you'll instead receive approximately $54,000 per annum, and your spouse will then receive $27,000 per annum during their lifetime.

COLA, when applicable, is based on *your* pension payout; if you choose to take the life-only option, you will get COLA on the higher amount. The additional $6,000 per year, along with the higher COLA, can potentially add up to hundreds of thousands of additional dollars in income during your retirement years.

Remember also that if you are retiring prior to age 55, you will not receive COLA adjustments from your pension until after you reach that age. The length of your service also affects COLA; if you have less than 15 years of service, your COLA will be tied to the annual change in the Consumer Price Index (CPI),[77] rather than receiving the flat 3 percent adjustment used for members with longer terms of service.

Tend To Surviving Spouse Benefits

Good news. Keep in mind that no matter what payout option you select for your surviving spouse, they will receive an additional Statutory Retirement benefit every month. As of 2019, this monthly benefit is $875.60 and increases annually in July by $16.50.

The best thing you can do here is to just keep score. Make sure there is a recorded, updated annual of the additional expected benefit. This attention to detail will be appreciated by your family, further on down the road.

Use Life Insurance As Pension Payoff Protection

Many police officers and firefighters opt to take the higher, life-only pension option and use part or all of the difference that would have been taken out under a joint plan to buy life insurance. Upon your death, proceeds from this insurance will pass, tax free, to your spouse, who can then either gain interest on the whole lump sum or choose to start withdrawing in smaller amounts. The proceeds can also be used to purchase any other type of investment, which can then be passed on to other beneficiaries, children, or grandchildren upon the spouse's death.

Want to instead keep that additional $6,000 per year to spend? Use the dividends, or income, from a well-structured investment portfolio to pay the insurance premiums, and then you can keep and spend your pension check.

Choosing the correct type of life insurance is critical to the success of this strategy; the well-being of your spouse and loved ones depends on it. There are many nuances to different types of life insurance, and a simple mistake may cost your family a lot of money. But a properly structured "private pension" can generate a tax free lump sum "supplemental payment" to your spouse that can also be stretched to other beneficiaries. Don't forget, when you and your spouse pass, a traditional pension payout will not leave anything for your children.

OHIO Police & Fire: Sample Single Life Versus 50% Joint & Survivor Pension Payout	
$5,000 / Month	
Year	Pension Benefits under Single Life Option*
1	$60,000.00
5	$67,200.00
10	$76,200.00
15	$85,200.00
20	$94,200.00
25	$103,200.00
30	$112,200.00
TOTAL	**$2,583,000.00**
$4,500 / Month	
Year	Pension Benefits under 50% Joint & Survivor Option*
1	$54,000.00
5	$60,480.00
10	$68,580.00
15	$76,680.00
20	$84,780.00
25	$92,880.00
30	$100,980.00
TOTAL	**$2,324,700.00**
Difference in Annual Benefits with COLA at 3%	**$258,300.00**
*Assumes Member was at least age 55 upon retirement.	

Table O

Make The Most Of Survivor Pensions

Survivor pensions are available to eligible survivors of an active or retired police officer or firefighter who was a member of OP&F. Pensions are also available to eligible survivors if the date of death was within one year of the member's termination or leave of absence.

Surviving spouses who remarry will continue to receive the monthly survivor's benefit. Please note that a surviving spouse is eligible to receive a reduced benefit of only $410 per month if he or she is also receiving a full death benefit payable under the Ohio Public Safety Officers Death Benefit Fund statute. Also note that these numbers may well change in the coming years; please consult your plan administrator or your Financial Quarterback for the most up-to-date numbers. OP&F also has a brochure about the Death Benefit Fund[78] available on their website.

Any surviving children under the age of 18 are also eligible for a monthly pension of $234.30 in 2019, which increases annually in July by $4.50. Children become ineligible for this benefit upon reaching age 18, or in the event of marriage or death. Disabled children may be eligible to receive benefits beyond age 18, depending on the severity of the disability.

Maximize Social Security Benefits

Examine your job history to determine if the Windfall Elimination Provision (WEP) may affect you. If you have 30 or more years of "substantial" earnings in a job where you paid Social Security taxes, you might be able to eliminate an offset by as much as 67 percent of your Social Security benefits, up to as much as $480 (as of 2020). Every year has to be accounted for, and you *must* follow the Social Security tables, which can be found online or provided by your Financial Quarterback.

Be aware, too, of how the Government Pension Offset (GPO) may affect your Social Security. If you receive a federal, state, or local government pension based on work where you did not pay Social Security taxes, but you are also eligible for Social Security from other employment, your survivor's Social Security benefits may be reduced. For more specifics on WEP and GPO, refer back to chapter 10.

Health Insurance: A Whole New Ball Game

OP&F will no longer sponsor a self-funded healthcare program starting in 2019. In the announcement, Executive Director John Gallagher[79] added, "We are still committed to assisting members [to] find an appropriate healthcare plan." Why the dramatic change? Because projections showed that if OP&F maintained its current level of coverage, its $900 million healthcare fund will be drained within nine years, leaving all 58,000 members in health peril.

So what does this mean exactly, for both the short and long-term? There are many unknowns for the future of OP&F healthcare. Even those who are struggling to get the best deal for retirees in their system are not sure what the next few years may hold. But there is one thing for certain: *healthcare expenses can CRUSH retirement dreams.* Fidelity Investments estimates that, as of 2019, the average retired couple aged 65 may need to have approximately $285,000 saved, after tax, to cover healthcare expenses that may occur over the course of their retirement.

OP&F does plan to preserve some level of healthcare for their retirees for a period of 15 years. This makes for an uncertain reality for the 58,000 current and retired police officers and firefighters, all of who were expecting the system to remain intact for the duration of their lives.

Given the dramatic change in the healthcare process and the need for a substantial rainy-day fund, we urge you to understand the details of the new system, so you can make sure to take the proper next steps to plan for today and tomorrow. And, when necessary, seek knowledgeable guidance.

The New Stipend System Basics

The new system will likely seem complex to members, as it's so different from what they're used to. Don't be afraid to reach out to your benefits counselor to get help navigating this system. Here is a summary of some of the basics.

Under the new system, OP&F members will receive a fixed-cost monthly stipend via a Health Reimbursement Account (HRA) that can be used to pay for various medical costs. In order to have access to that stipend, members must have an account with the Aon Retiree Health Exchange.[80] Through this health exchange and their enrollment partner, members can access various options for an Individual & Family health-care plan sold through licensed insurance agents. Keep in mind that for Medicare eligible participants, plans are offered through Aon. However, for Pre-Medicare participants, plans are offered through eHealth.[81]

Members can dictate how the premiums will be paid and how much will come out of their own pockets, and they will have the option to leave money in the HRA to pay for copays and other out-of-pocket expenses. Most of the time, any amount going toward insurance premiums will be paid directly out of the HRA account; the money does not pass through the member's hands directly, and is therefore not taxable.

Any money left in the HRA account at the end of the year is forfeit; it will not roll over for the following year.

At the time of retirement from an OP&F job, the member has 60 days to enroll in the new plan. They also have the option of enrolling in a spouse's plan, but if they do that, they will not have the option again to enter the new OP&F plan unless a qualifying event (marriage, death, divorce, the involuntary loss of group coverage, or the date of Medicare eligibility) takes place. If such an event occurs, the member has 60 days to enroll.

Spouses who are not on their own healthcare plan have the option of joining the OP&F plan, but those who have a different plan cannot enroll unless there is a qualifying event. Certain dependents may be eligible as well. The plan also has a survivorship aspect, allowing the spouse to be on the plan after the death of the OP&F member.

OP&F will be revisiting this plan on an annual basis, and there is always a possibility of the stipend amounts changing to reflect new circumstances.

2020 OP&F Retiree Healthcare Plan Monthly Stipend Levels					
	Medicare Status		Monthly Medical/Rx Stipend	Monthly Medicare Part B Reimbursement*	Total OP&F Monthly Support For Health Care
	Retiree	Spouse			
Retiree Only:	Medicare		$143	$107	$250
	Non- Medicare		$685	$0	$685
Retiree + Spouse:	Medicare	Medicare	$239	$107	$346
	Medicare	Non-Medicare	$525	$107	$632
	Non-Medicare	Medicare	$788	$0	$788
	Non-Medicare	Non-Medicare	$1,074	$0	$1,074
Retiree + Dependents:	Medicare		$203	$107	$310
	Non- Medicare		$865	$0	$865
Retiree + Spouse + Dependents:	Medicare	Either Medicare or	$525	$107	$632
	Non- Medicare	Non- Medicare	$1,074	$0	$1,074
Surviving Spouse:	Medicare		$143	$107	$250
	Non- Medicare		$685	$0	$685

*The OP&F Medicare Part B reimbursement is an ongoing benefit that has been in place for many years, but should be included in the support provided for healthcare coverage. The Med B reimbursement is added to a member's monthly pension benefit, adapted from OP&F site.

Table P

Disability Benefits

A member can apply for disability benefits within one year of being placed on administrative leave or terminating their employment. To be eligible, you must either still be making contributions to OP&F or your past contributions must have remained on deposit. If you're a participant in DROP, you cannot also qualify for disability benefits. Termination of active service at any time during the process of applying for disability will render that application null and void. It will also immediately vest a DROP benefit.

There are two types of disability: service-incurred (on-the-job) or non-service-incurred (off-duty). To be eligible for benefits in either type, the disability must be permanent. If the disability is service-incurred, there is no minimum period of service required to qualify for benefits.

Service-incurred disabilities can be further divided into two categories; *permanent and total*, or *partial*. *Permanent and total* disability means that you are unable to perform either your official police or fire duties or the duties of any occupation for which you might otherwise be prepared to do via your past experience or education, and currently it does not look like you will ever recover.

The annual benefit for a permanent and total disability is 72 percent of your average annual salary. For OP&F members with 15 years of service or more as of July 1, 2013, this is an average of the three years of highest allowable earnings. For members with less than 15 years of service credit as of July 1, 2013, this would be the average of the five years of highest allowable earnings. Your average annual salary includes salary, earnings, or compensation, regardless of when in your career the highest years occurred, but is subject to certain statutory and administrative limitations. Therefore, not all salary, earnings, or compensation will necessarily be used in the calculation.

A *partial* disability means that you are disabled to the extent that you are unable to perform your official police or fire duties and your earnings capacity is therefore diminished. However, it is assumed that you are capable and willing to obtain another form of employment and supplement your disability benefit that way.

If you have less than 25 years of service credit, the annual benefit payable under a partial disability grant is set by the OP&F Board of Trustees to be a certain percentage of your average annual salary, as explained above. The maximum percentage that the Board can award an individual with less than 25 years of service is 60 percent of that average salary. If you do have 25 years or more, then OP&F's Board of Trustees will determine your partial disability. The amount of the annual benefit is set by law to be equal to your normal service retirement pension. However, it can't exceed 72 percent of your average annual salary. To calculate your annual benefit, you can multiply the average annual salary by a percentage equal to 60 percent, and then add 1.5 percent for each year of service from 26 to 33. For example, 28 years of service would mean you would receive 64.5 percent of your annual average salary.

If your disabling condition isn't job-related and you're an eligible OP&F member, you may meet the requirements for a non-service-incurred disability benefit, provided that you have at least five years of service credit. Additionally, it's important to note that you may be able to purchase or restore service credit in order to meet this five-year requirement.

In order to be eligible for this kind of off-duty disability benefit, the disability must prevent you from performing official duties and impair your earnings ability. The annual benefit is set by OP&F's Board of Trustees to be a certain percentage of your average annual salary, but cannot exceed 60 percent.

OP&F provides an entire guide regarding their disability processes, and this section should only serve as a summary of the basics. To more fully understand the disability guidelines, I encourage you to access the pension fund's guide online and download for future reference.

Do-It-Yourself, Or Do It With Professional Help?

With all the changes, we respectfully suggest you get the advice of a market-proven Financial Quarterback to help you make the right health insurance choices, and to help you ensure that those choices are seamlessly coordinated with your other retirement assets. You've worked hard, and you deserve to have a secure retirement laid out ahead of you.

Aside from the fact that the costs of hiring such a financial planner are negligible, ultimately, good financial advisors will pay for themselves. The choice is yours; the only advice we can give to the determined do-it-yourselfer is don't be pennywise and *pound foolish.*

•   •   •

SUMMARY: Chapter 15

- Peace of mind in retirement is UP TO YOU. Use every resource at your disposal to maximize retirement benefits and choose the right plans to protect yourself from medical catastrophe.
- If you're over age 50, use catch-up contributions to reduce taxes.
- Consider utilizing DROP to accumulate a lump sum in retirement. Weigh it against any promotion or increases you may receive between then and retiring.
- Expand your investment portfolio; discover different options for 403(b) and 457(b) retirement plans.
- There are a variety of single and joint survivor payout options to choose from; know your options and make the best selection for you.
- Consider using life insurance in place of a joint survivor option.
- Analyze all of your options for survivor pensions and configure them in a way that won't unexpectedly create a hardship.
- Know how WEP & GPO may affect the Social Security benefits for you and your loved ones.
- OP&F recently made a huge change to their healthcare benefits, switching to a stipend-based system. Understand these latest changes and know how they'll affect you and your family.
- Discuss your situation with your Financial Quarterback and others such as a tax attorney to help ensure you are meeting your retirement needs and protecting your estate/loved ones when you are gone.

16

SERS:
STATE EMPLOYEE
RETIREMENT SYSTEM

embers of the State Employee Retirement System (SERS) are the unsung heroes of the Ohio public school system. Although you may not be as recognized as teaching staff in general, you perform important responsibilities that keep schools running smoothly, the student experience conducive to learning, and the learning environment safe. Part of the reward for the top service you provide is SERS membership and access to SERS[82] programs. These programs include one of the strongest retirement systems in public service. SERS also provides its members with significant financial tools for retirement, savings, and healthcare, along with solid support for all its members.

In 2018, SERS had 237,138 active and retired members. As the 61st largest public pension fund in the country, SERS holds $13.6 billion in assets.

• • •

Plan Options

SERS does not offer the same number of plans as OPERS, STRS, and some of the other Ohio public pension funds. Instead, there is a single plan, which is similar in many ways to the Combined Plans offered by both OPERS and STRS. As a member, you are essentially funding your retirement through employee and employer contributions, as well as investment returns on these contributions.

The retirement eligibility requirement SERS implemented in August 2017 covers two types of retirement: unreduced service retirement, and early service retirement with reduced benefits.

Members with 25 years of service are eligible to retire with unreduced benefits either at age 65 with 5 years of service credits, or at any age with 30 years of service credits. Members with less than 25 years of service as of August 1, 2017, can receive unreduced service retirement at age 67 with 10 years of service credits, or age 57 with 30 years.

For early service retirement with reduced benefits, members with at least 25 years of service as of August 1, 2017, are eligible to retire at age 60 with 5 years, or age 55 with 25 years. Members with less than 25 years of experience on that same date can retire at age 62 with 10 years, or age 60 with 25 years.

If you have more than one job with a SERS employer, you are able to retire from the highest paying position and continue working in the lower-paying position. In the example offered on the pension fund's website, if you are a custodian and a bus driver and have two distinct salaries, those salaries will both be used in the calculation of your pension, and you can keep working in the lowest-paying job after you retire. You must have distinct salaries or individual contracts, or work for more than one SERS employer to do this.

If you work under Ohio Public Employees Retirement System (OPERS) or State Teachers Retirement System (STRS) in addition to SERS, you may be able to retire from the highest paying position and continue in the lower-paying job. If you continue in the lower-paying position after you retire, you will be a reemployed retiree. Your original pension will not be affected by continuing to work in this lower-paying position.

Your pension is based on age, service credit, and salary. The age used in a pension calculation is your actual age at the time you retire. If you plan to retire July 1, but your birthday is July 15, it may be a good idea to postpone your retirement date until August 1. However, you would lose that month's pension check, so it may not be worth it.

Formula:
Age + Service Credit + Salary = Pension.

A comparison of the "before" and "after" estimates will help you make the right decision. Keep in mind that all your service credit will be used in calculating your pension benefit. It is possible to purchase service credits, but they must be purchased before your retirement date. Working with an advisor or the staff at SERS is the best way to look at all the scenarios involved and make the best decision for you and your family. It's not uncommon to recover the cost of purchasing service credits in two or three years by receiving a higher pension.

Disability Benefits

If you become disabled while employed, you may be eligible for benefits under one of two plans. These are the same plans discussed in an earlier chapter about OPERS (Chapter 13).

The eligibility rules for disability include:

1. Have at least five years of total service credit.
2. File an application no later than two years from the date that your contributing service stopped.
3. Are permanently disabled, either physically or mentally, for work in your SERS-covered position as determined by a physician appointed by SERS.
4. Became disabled after becoming a SERS member.
5. Did not receive a refund of your contributions.
6. Do not receive a service retirement benefit.

You are not eligible to apply for a SERS disability benefit if you are receiving a disability benefit from another Ohio retirement system: no double dipping. You also cannot apply for a SERS disability benefit if your condition resulted from a felony act or occurred after your SERS-covered employment ended.

Healthcare

Any SERS member with at least 10 years of qualified service credit is eligible for healthcare coverage. Dental and vision coverage is also available. To receive dental and vision, you must meet eligibility requirements but do not necessarily need to be enrolled in SERS healthcare coverage. Keep in mind that when you retire, you cannot waive SERS' healthcare coverage in order to enroll in coverage from another Ohio public retirement system.

All members pay premiums for healthcare coverage, which covers medical care and prescription drugs. Premiums are based on years of qualified service credit, eligibility for subsidies, and the healthcare plan selected. SERS automatically deducts your premiums from your monthly benefit payment.

SERS also offers a subsidy for premiums. To qualify for a subsidy, you must have at least 20 years of qualified service credit or be receiving a disability benefit. In addition, at the time of retirement, disability, or separation, you must be eligible to participate in the health plan of your last employer, or have been eligible to participate in the health plan of your last employer at least three of the last five years.

SERS offers two non-Medicare plans, as well as the option for a SERS Marketplace Wraparound Plan,[83] which works in combination with the health insurance marketplace. The SERS Marketplace Wraparound Plan provides additional benefits to help pay for deductibles, copays, and other medical costs, and there is no additional premium. There are, however, eligibility requirements.

Manage Health Insurance Costs

When you retire, you and any eligible dependents will have the option to participate in the SERS-sponsored healthcare plan. This plan includes medical, prescription drugs, dental, and vision plans for qualifying retirees.

You are eligible to enroll in SERS health coverage under these circumstances:

1. When you retire or begin to receive disability.
2. Within 90 days of becoming eligible for Medicare.
3. Within 31 days of involuntary termination of other healthcare coverage or Medicaid.

If your spouse or other dependents were not enrolled during the initial enrollment, you may enroll them under any of the following circumstances:

- Within 31 days of marriage.
- Within 31 days of birth or adoption.
- Within 90 days of your spouse becoming eligible for Medicare.
- Within 31 days of involuntary termination of the healthcare coverage of your spouse or child (26 or younger).

The premiums for SERS healthcare coverage are deducted from your monthly benefit check.

Alternative Retirement Plans (ARPs)

College employees may have the option to participate in an Alternative Retirement Plan (ARP) as an alternative to the normal SERS plan. ARPs can vary significantly, and the best information available will come from your organization, or possibly a third-party vendor. When making the choice, keep in mind that it's irrevocable as long as you're continuously employed.

Learn More

There's so much more to the various aspects of SERS membership than we can reasonably cover in this book. If you're a member or curious to learn more, please spend some time exploring the SERS website, where you can find out more about the various details of your plan, including eligibility and healthcare requirements.

Making The Most Of SERS Contributions

Along with your employer, you are required to contribute a percentage of your compensation to SERS to fund your retirement benefits. Your share of the contribution is 10 percent of gross compensation; your employer pays 14 percent. Gross compensation does not include pay for unused sick or vacation time, but does include regular vacation time, sick leave, and overtime.

Should you terminate your job before qualifying for a SERS retirement, you may request a refund for only the amount of *your* contributions and the purchase of any service credit. A smart move would be to immediately roll these refunds into a qualified retirement account such as an IRA; otherwise, you will be taxed and possibly penalized by the IRS.

Maximize Tax Reduction Pre-Retirement

One of the first items on your list to maximize your retirement should be to try to take advantage of the catch-up contributions. The IRS allows individuals who are age 50 and over to make additional retirement contributions to their qualified retirement plans (403[b] or 457[b]).

These contributions will lower your tax bill, as they are pre-tax in the year that you make them. The money will continue to grow, tax deferred, until distributed.

Any money put away now under these IRS provisions is money available in retirement as a lump sum, or to supplement your monthly retirement income. In most plans, you need not touch any of this money until you're 72. See Chapter 7 for a more in-depth discussion.

Rules Permitting IRA Contributions

You may be eligible for other helpful retirement vehicles such as traditional and ROTH IRAs, and it's worth considering if they make sense for your individual tax, family, or legacy situation. These plans are not technically part of your employer benefits, but maximizing savings in IRA options may also be helpful for a comfortable retirement. The after-tax contribution and tax free withdrawal of a ROTH IRA make it particularly interesting should future tax rates rise.

IRAs and Roth IRAs are covered in depth in Chapter 8.

Social Security Coordination

As we discussed in earlier chapters, the rules for collecting SERS and Social Security often confuse people. The first thing you need to know is that if you don't pay into Social Security for 40 fiscal quarters, you will pay substantially higher Medicare Part A and B premiums in the future.

Ohio state and local government employees may also be hurt by two rules that affect their ability to receive their entire Social Security benefit. The first is called the Government Pension Offset (GPO); the second is called the Windfall Elimination Provision (WEP). These two rules are covered in depth in Chapter 10.

If you have been paying into the system, you can start receiving benefits as early as age 62 or as late as age 70. For every month that you begin to collect before full retirement age (see the table in Chapter 10), your Social Security benefit will be reduced for the rest of your life. This is often a tricky decision, and one that should not be made without careful consideration.

Purchasing Service Credits

Service credits are one of the primary measurements that determine when a member is eligible for retirement as well as how much of a benefit amount they are entitled to under both traditional pension and combined plans. Total service credit includes both the length of time you have actually contributed service and earned "time" as well as any credits that have been *purchased* through the system in order to reduce necessary time until retirement eligibility.

Service credits can also be purchased for other types of service, including out-of-state federal service, military service, leaves of absence, and services that were exempt. Purchasing service is done through a form you can obtain online. Service credits are also covered in more depth in Chapter 9.

Under the SERS-defined benefit plan, the full amount is determined by a combination of eligibility calculation and the amount of retirement payout. One year of service credit may be granted for completion of 120 days or more of school employment in Ohio.

The fiscal school year runs from July 1 through June 30. If your service is less than 120 days, SERS will grant a fraction of a year's credit. This fraction is determined by dividing the number of days by 180. As little as one hour in a workday will entitle you to purchase one day of service. Use Table Q on the following page to determine the fractional service you are entitled to purchase.

Under most situations, it is advisable to take advantage of as many opportunities to purchase service credits as possible. You may even use existing IRA, 403(b), and 457 funds for this purpose.

	Fractional Service Credit For Year When Working Less Than 120 Days										
Days	Percent	Days	Percent	Days	Percent	Days	Percent	Days	Percent	Days	Percent
1	.006	21	.117	41	.228	61	.339	81	.450	101	.561
2	.011	22	.122	42	.233	62	.344	82	.456	102	.567
3	.017	23	.128	43	.239	63	.350	83	.461	103	.572
4	.022	24	.133	44	.244	64	.356	84	.467	104	.578
5	.028	25	.139	45	.250	65	.361	85	.472	105	.583
6	.033	26	.144	46	.256	66	.367	86	.478	106	.589
7	.039	27	.150	47	.261	67	.372	87	.483	107	.594
8	.044	28	.156	48	.267	68	.378	88	.489	108	.600
9	.050	29	.161	49	.272	69	.383	89	.494	109	.606
10	.056	30	.167	50	.278	70	.389	90	.500	110	.611
11	.061	31	.172	51	.283	71	.394	91	.506	111	.617
12	.067	32	.178	52	.289	72	.400	92	.511	112	.622
13	.072	33	.183	53	.294	73	.406	93	.517	113	.628
14	.078	34	.189	54	.300	74	.411	94	.522	114	.633
15	.083	35	.194	55	.306	75	.417	95	.528	115	.639
16	.089	36	.200	56	.311	76	.422	96	.533	116	.644
17	.094	37	.206	57	.317	77	.428	97	.539	117	.650
18	.100	38	.211	58	.322	78	.433	98	.544	118	.656
19	.106	39	.217	59	.328	79	.439	99	.550	119	.611
20	.111	40	.222	60	.333	80	.444	100	.556	120	1.000

Table Q

Partial Lump Sum Option Plan

Another exciting option is the Partial Lump Sum Option Plan (PLOP). This allows retiring plan participants to immediately receive a lump sum, which is "carved" from your pension, in addition to a reduced monthly benefit payment. The chosen lump sum is at the discretion of the employee, but it cannot be less than 6 times or more than 36 times the monthly amount that would be collected under traditional pension payments.

Essentially, your lump sum upon retirement may be up to three years' worth of payment in one check, but no less than a month-and-a-half's worth. The amount taken will reduce your monthly payment going forward according to a complex formula. Greater discussion of PLOP can be found starting in Chapter 13.

SUMMARY: Chapter 16

- If you leave your job before qualifying for retirement, you can receive a refund on contributions taken from your paycheck.
- If you're over 50, you can make additional contributions to qualified retirement plans.
- Are traditional or ROTH IRAs a good fit for you?
- Examine the SERS-sponsored healthcare plan to understand when to enroll and what is covered.
- Examine WEP & GPO to see if they apply to your situation. The younger you take Social Security, the smaller your monthly check.
- Determine if you can purchase service credits for other work or positions you've had in state or government employment.
- SERS allows retirees to opt for a partial lump sum at retirement.
- Discuss your situation with your Financial Quarterback and others such as a tax attorney to help ensure you are meeting your retirement needs and protecting your estate/loved ones when you are gone.

17

HPRS: HIGHWAY PATROL RETIREMENT SYSTEM

T he State Highway Patrol is the division of the Ohio Department of Public Safety tasked with keeping Ohio's roadways safe, protecting the governor and dignitaries, providing emergency response services, and supporting the overall allied criminal justice fraternity. The ranks swell at times and contract at times, but the Highway Patrol maintains an overall force of roughly 1,600 uniformed officers and 1,000 support personnel.

There are many character values sought after during the recruiting process, and these values are reinforced and encouraged through membership in the Highway Patrol. These values include professionalism, adaptability, urgency, and a strong sense of safety. This is obviously not a complete list of traits, but these *are* some of the attributes that may also need to be called upon as members review their retirement options.

As budgetary pressure mounts to reduce retirement benefits, members of the Highway Patrol Retirement System (HPRS)[84] have a unique set of options that, when taken together with their values, should lead toward success as they disconnect from service. This chapter discusses the details and options available to HPRS members along with some planning considerations to make before making any important decisions.

Retirement Benefit Health

HPRS retirees currently have access to healthcare, but this benefit is not required by state law. Premiums and coverage available to members change annually; annual open enrollment is during the month of November.

The HPRS investment portfolio is growing, and returns for the six years proceeding and through 2017 have averaged above the "typical" return target of 7.5 to 8 percent.

HPRS Investment Returns		
Date	Investment Portfolio Market Value	YTD Increase/ Decrease
09/12/2019	$892,400,000 est.	11.5% est.
03/16/2018	$912,000,000 est.	1.80% est.
12/31/2017	$902,452,000	14.40%
12/31/2016	$825,505,000	7.30%
12/31/2015	$809,209,000	(0.30%)
12/31/2014	$849,000,000	6.50%
12/31/2013	$813,953,000	19.60%

Table R

HPRS members who are currently nearing the end of their career can be confident that they will not be affected by any major changes to their plan. The HPRS retirement plan includes some unique options that allow the retiring worker to either become more self-reliant on investment success, to depend solely on the defined benefit from HPRS, or to custom design a combination of both.

I use many financial strategies in my practice to help the affluent. But these strategies are helpful to everyone; under most scenarios, proper planning can take you further than you had anticipated. Using tools outside your employer's plan to tailor your own personalized retirement strategy means you effectively have both a belt *and* suspenders for the future. If one fails, the other is still there to make sure you don't get caught in a difficult situation.

A solid Financial Quarterback, especially one with extensive experience in the benefits of state employees, can help you achieve this kind of security. Remember that, in the long run, the costs are negligible; ultimately, good financial advisors pay for themselves.

Taxes Pre-Retirement

Are you doing everything you can to reduce the amount of taxes you pay prior to retirement?

If you're over age 50, you may increase the amount of your tax deferred savings via catch-up contributions to qualified accounts. As most people expect to live another 25 to 40 years, placing additional savings in tax deferred savings now will reduce the taxes you pay in the current year, and the money will compound tax deferred until distributed. See Chapter 7 for more information on catch-up contributions.

Are you maximizing the use of your 457(b) plan? Your Ohio-deferred compensation 457(b) plan allows you to make extra payments, the mechanism for which was discussed at greater length in Chapter 6. These contributions can be pre-tax and grow tax deferred. As an added bonus, the funds in your 457(b) plan may be used to purchase service credit for your HPRS pension.

You should also be aware of—and take advantage of—the traditional IRA and Roth IRA contributions that make the most sense for your particular tax, family, and legacy situation. While these are not technically part of your pension benefits, you will appreciate having maximized the amounts of any IRA accounts you might hold further down the road. See Chapter 8 for more about IRAs.

Deferred Retirement Option Plan (DROP)

This is a benefit available to HPRS members that allows the accumulation of tax deferred savings that will be paid as a lump sum after retirement. The accumulation is within the pension design, which ultimately guarantees principal under the state of Ohio.

There are numerous restrictions and conditions that must be met prior to being allowed to contribute to a DROP plan. First among them is you'll need to have already purchased all prior years of service. You must participate for three to eight years if you have not reached age 52; if you're over age 53, you must participate for two to eight years or until you've reached your 60th birthday.

One of the considerations of using DROP is that it locks in the amount of your pension; if you were to get promoted during or after accumulation in DROP, your lifetime pension will not benefit from any pay increase caused by the promotion. In most situations, it is advisable for officers and support staff to take any and all overtime possibilities offered prior to enrolling in the DROP plan. Doing this helps increase your average wage during the time that counts toward your pension payout. Should a member die while enrolled in the DROP plan, the proceeds of the plan will be paid to either the surviving spouse or to the member's estate.

Partial Lump Sum (PLUS)

The PLUS option allows participants to elect to withdraw a larger portion of funds from their pension account at the beginning of retirement for immediate use (fully taxable in the year withdrawn, and other IRS levies may apply), or to rollover into a qualified plan such as an IRA or a retirement annuity. This will, in turn, reduce the member's monthly payout for life.

In order to be eligible for PLUS at retirement, a member must have reached age 51 with a minimum of 25 years' service, or age 52 with at least 20 years of service. The lump sum received may not be less than six times the monthly single life pension, and it is capped at 60 times the monthly payment (or the equivalent of five years). This option is compatible with both Single Life and Joint and Survivor options.

Disability

Like in OP&F, members of HPRS may be eligible for disability benefits whether their disability is incurred in the line of duty or otherwise. If you are disabled due to an injury or illness determined to be job related, you're entitled to a minimum pension benefit of 61.25 percent of your final average salary (FAS). The Pension Factor (PF) is calculated as though you have 25 years of full-time active service with the OSHP. If you have more than 25 years of service, the additional service credit will be calculated into the PF.

If you are disabled due to an injury or illness that is not job related, you're entitled to a minimum pension benefit of 30 percent of your FAS, with the PF calculated as though you have at least 12 years of full-time, active service with the OSHP. If you have more than 12 years, that will also be calculated into the PF. Keep in mind that eligibility requires that you have at least five years of qualifying HPRS service credit.

No matter how your disability was incurred, any member receiving disability benefits is required by law to supply annual information related to their disability status, as well as information about current employment status (if applicable). It's also important to note that all disability pensions offered are single life annuities.

Survivor Pensions

Survivor pensions are available to eligible beneficiaries of HPRS members. As of 2020, surviving spouses of retired members who are not eligible for retirement will receive $911.25 per month, with COLA, increases being added annually based on board votes. Although an increase is not guaranteed, surviving spouses with dependent children will receive an additional $150 per month until the child reaches either age 18 or 23, depending on their student status. This eligibility is reviewed by the board on a case-by-case basis to determine the duration that benefits will be provided. (Lifetime benefits are only available for disabled children. The board will determine the severity of the disability and then determine how long the benefit will be paid out).

A surviving spouse of a member who either retired or entered DROP before May 11, 2018, will receive an amount equal to either 50 percent of the retiree's pension benefit or $900 per month, whichever is greater. If the member retired or entered DROP after that date, the surviving spouse will receive $911.25 per month (as of 2019), with COLA increases set by the board. This survivor benefit is in addition to any amount selected through a Joint and Survivor Annuity (JSA).

What To Do Now

Before deciding on when to retire, take the time to find out how much money you will need monthly (after taxes and insurance) to enjoy a comfortable living. A well-thought-out plan that incorporates legal considerations, tax implications, and asset maximization for beneficiaries is an important first step. You may even be able to tailor a unique strategy specifically for your situation, such as combining DROP, a "pension max," and the purchase of life insurance, with a PLUS option. This is just one of many examples of a customized solution that can help to maximize your retirement benefits, but it needs to be handled by someone who really understands the ins and outs of all your benefits! An experienced Financial Quarterback can help you run the numbers and develop a customized plan that's right for you.

SUMMARY: Chapter 17

- Highway Patrol Officers shouldn't count on their current healthcare benefits remaining unchanged until they're ready to retire. Currently, retirees have access to healthcare, but that isn't required by state law and it may change.
- With DROP, you can work past your normal retirement age and receive an extra lump sum when you do finally retire.
- Review the option of taking a partial lump sum at retirement. Consider rolling your PLUS lump sum into an IRA to broaden your investment options and possibly leave benefits for your surviving family.
- Any survivors of members of HPRS may be eligible for a survivor pension, whether the member was retired or not.
- Analyze your current situation and tailor a plan to suit your needs.
- Discuss your situation with your Financial Quarterback and others such as a tax attorney to help ensure you are meeting your retirement needs and protecting your estate/loved ones when you are gone.

SECTION 4

HOW TO PLAN
FOR RETIREMENT

18

DEVELOP THE RIGHT BUCKET LIST

I f you are reading this book, you are no doubt thinking about planning your own retirement. Chances are good you will have, on average, 18 years in retirement—maybe even longer. So, figuring out just how to prepare is a bit more complicated than it used to be. But it always starts in the same place. If you're ready to get started, here are some first steps to take.[85]

1. Have Clear, Mutually Agreed-Upon Goals

I've noticed during the past 25 years that when prospective clients first come to me, many have done a decent job of saving money but most haven't taken the time to set any tangible goals for retirement. Often, what ideas they have are half-baked, fuzzy, or nonexistent. Not surprisingly, they have no *strategy* to support these nonexistent goals.

Goals need to be specific. "Travel more" is not a goal. "Visit Saint Petersburg," "Celebrate Oktoberfest in Munich," or "ride the three largest roller coasters in the U.S." *are* goals. A specific goal promotes action;

with a specific goal, you can develop a strategy and determine how best to accomplish it. If your goals are fuzzy, your plans will be fuzzy, too.

It's important to think clearly about what you want and bring these goals into the light. With exploration, retirees may discover that other activities they choose to do in retirement are in direct conflict with their goals.

As an example, a woman who had been teaching history for 22 years finally retired. Five years into her retirement, she shared with me that she had once planned to spend a month exploring Asia, perhaps even walk the length of the Great Wall of China. When I asked why she hadn't yet taken that trip, the woman, a widow, told me that retirement left her feeling a bit alone, so she had decided to adopt a dachshund. And that required her to be home more.

Raising a pet is a valid goal and undertaking, but it had never previously been one of hers. What to do? Her dachshund was now her "close partner," obviously filling a need for companionship. Getting rid of a beloved pet is not an option. What we could do, however, was to figure out a cost-effective way for her to arrange for care for the dog while she traveled. At the same time, we also eliminated some other concerns of hers so that she could take her trip before she became too old to hike the Great Wall.

Understanding your goals, knowing the location of your end zone, is important. You don't want to be running in the opposite direction for too long and learn you've lost too many yards. Because when you finally realize that, it may be too late; you haven't done anything you've wanted and suddenly it's too late to get started.

2. Determine How Much You Will Need

Take the time to find out how much money you will need on a monthly basis (after taxes and insurance) to enjoy a comfortable retirement. Your best and most important first step is a well-thought-out plan that incorporates legal considerations, tax implications, and asset maximization for beneficiaries. There may even be a unique strategy specifically tailored for your situation, but you can't work out a strategy until you begin to lay out the numbers.

Couples should begin discussing their dreams with each other long before they hand in their respective ID cards on their last days of work. You may be assuming you and your other half are gearing up for the same dream, only to find out later that you've been working against one other. You've wasted time when you should have been clearing a path for both of you to achieve your individual and joint goals.

Retirement does not often look as it's depicted in advertisements. Magazine and television ads show whirlwind travel and major life changes, but this is not the reality for most. This vision often has the effect of scaring people into believing they can't retire until they can afford this level of luxury. The truth is, most people focus more on hobbies and rearranging and repairing their "nest" in retirement than they do on big expenses.[86] The cost of recreation is often far less than many thought it would be in retirement. In fact, many of these costs actually decrease.

Once you have come up with your retirement budget, try and live on it for 6 to 12 months and see how it works. If it is too tight and doesn't afford you the lifestyle you want, there is nothing wrong with adjusting the plan and working a little longer to pay down some more debt or accumulate more money. It's much easier to make these adjustments while you are still working than it is to find out *after* you retire, which may force you to find another job to achieve the lifestyle you want.

3. Cultivate Good Lifestyle Habits Now And For Later

One of the best pre-retirement health plans doesn't cost money, it requires good habits. It's called a good night's sleep. And it's designed to help you prepare mentally and physically with the inevitable challenges of aging.

Between 2003 and 2017, the University of Pennsylvania conducted the "American Time Use Survey"[87] with more than 125,000 respondents in the United States. This study returned some very interesting conclusions. One important fact is that researchers found that workers who slept six or fewer hours per night worked, on average, 1.55 more hours each weekday and 1.86 more hours on weekends or holidays. This is in comparison to workers who slept more. The National Sleep Center recommends seven to nine hours per night for workers aged 26–64, and seven to eight hours for those over age 65.

A recent meta-analysis on occupational fatigue defines it as "a decreased ability to perform activities at the desired level due to lassitude or exhaustion of mental/or physical strength." This analysis concluded that inadequate amounts of sleep, along with work and environment factors, are "major drivers" of occupational fatigue. This fatigue hampers job performance and results in errors and injuries. According to the study, people who don't sleep well don't think as clearly, may not function as well physically, and may be more susceptible to illness. They may also have a "decreased ability to process and react to new information and respond to hazards." The bottom line? Make sure you get plenty of rest. This will pay dividends in retirement.

4. Take Advantage Of Health Savings Accounts (HSAs)

HSAs[88] have some interesting features. Understand them and use them wisely. Some quick facts:

- An HSA is a tax-deductible savings account used in conjunction with an HSA-qualified high-deductible health plan (HDHP).
- Contribution limits for 2020 are $3,550 for individuals and $7,100 for families.
- An HDHP is usually purchased through a state exchange.
- HSA funds are withdrawn to pay for qualified medical expenses. These withdrawals are tax- and penalty free.

5. Protect Assets Against Catastrophe

All is going well, and then it happens. Through no fault of your own, you find yourself in the middle of a lawsuit.

Did you know your income from IRAs and any deferred compensation plans may be at risk? Without the proper protections in place, a lot of your and your family's income from wages, pensions, and retirement accounts may be attachable in a settlement. Even with automobile and homeowner insurance, there are limits and deductibles on most policies, and the limits and deductibles of most policies mean these costs may not be covered. Fortunately, there are some relatively painless solutions. One might be to get an umbrella policy, which is a form of extra liability insurance coverage designed to protect against lawsuits.

How about your health? You may be under the impression that you and your family are adequately protected should either a serious illness occur or should long-term healthcare services become required, either at home or in a skilled nursing facility. You have Medicare Parts A, B, and D, plus your post-retirement state health benefits.

Between professional exclusions, spending maximums, out-of-pocket copays, the need for premium-priced branded drugs, and non-covered preexisting condition clauses, it is highly likely that all or the majority of a major hospital bill will put a big dent in your savings. A simple fall can necessitate a hip replacement and an extended hospital stay due to complications, and that combined with intensive physical therapy can cost hundreds of thousands of dollars that may not be covered by your insurance options.

Owning a long-term-care policy with a reputable, well-rated company can be a great way to possibly protect assets you wish to preserve or pass on. While these policies can be expensive to buy into, particularly if you wait until you are older, there are an increasing number of solutions that a knowledgeable financial professional can tailor to your situation.

Long-term-care products have also advanced over the years. Some older policies were essentially "use it or lose it" propositions where if you didn't use them, you'd lose all the premiums you paid over the years. More current policies can be attached to life insurance or annuities so that even if you never use the coverage, there may still be some benefits paid out to your loved ones if planned and structured properly.

6. Don't Overlook The Gap Years

Many police officers and firefighters choose to retire early, well before any Medicare benefits kick in. This time period between the beginning of retirement and the beginning of Medicare coverage (at age 65) is commonly called the *gap years*. Health insurance[89] can easily cost a family over $16,000 per year during these years when purchased through the retired member. It is critical to make proper allowances for this expenditure and to maximize choices in coverage options until you do finally qualify for Medicare.

Upon your retirement, if you are not yet eligible for Medicare, you and your qualifying dependents might be able to participate in your pension's sponsored healthcare plan. Speak with your benefits counselor to find out if this is an option for you. In this case, the healthcare premiums would be deducted directly from your monthly benefit check.

Depending on your situation, there are several other options for paying the substantial increase in out-of-pocket healthcare premiums during the gap years:

- Join your spouse's employee health plan as a family member.
- Work in a part-time job to cover the premium shortfall.
- Continue to work in a job that provides healthcare, even if you have to pay a supplemental premium to have the complete coverage you need.
- Determine (with the assistance of your Financial Quarterback) if your retirement assets can be invested properly and structured correctly to cover the entire gap between the lower premiums you paid when you worked full-time and the higher premiums after retirement.

- Operate a small business or work as an independent contractor in order to possibly deduct your healthcare premiums as a work expense.
- You may be able to purchase a plan on your state's exchange under the Affordable Care Act.

This is an issue that some people don't see coming. Make sure you have a plan.

7. Remain Vigilant About Your Pension Plan's Health Insurance Obligations

As mentioned earlier, healthcare will probably be your largest retirement expense. The connection between poor health and reduced wealth is very real. As a famous quote often erroneously attributed to the Dalai Lama[90] goes, "Man . . . sacrifices his health in order to make money. Then he sacrifices money to recuperate his health."

Ohio's five state employee pension systems are all required to provide members with a pension in exchange for fulfilling certain requirements. However, they are NOT required to provide you with healthcare. Healthcare is expensive, and the primary role of plan administrators is to keep those pension checks flowing, after all.

Remember:

- **OPERS** enacted dramatic price increases for its healthcare back in 2016. They currently calculate their healthcare fund will last indefinitely (Chapter 13).
- **STRS** indefinitely suspended its COLA as of 2017 in an effort to maintain healthcare coverage. The current healthcare fund is expected to be drained by 2035 (Chapter 14).
- **OP&F** has eliminated its healthcare plan and switched to a stipend-based system (Chapter 15).
- **SERS** is looking at a plan to cut COLA increases. The hope is that doing so will shore up the pension fund and

eventually free enough money to maintain healthcare coverage (Chapter 16).

- **HPRS** may be the smallest of the plans, but members have still faced premium hikes each year since 2011. It is projected that the fund will run out of money by 2026 (Chapter 17).

The only thing that seems certain about healthcare is that costs keep rising. *Doing nothing is not an option!* The most realistic solution is to face the problem head-on, utilizing solid investment solutions and putting away extra funds a bit more prudently to protect you and your family against future frustration with medical costs.

SUMMARY: Chapter 18

- Identify you and your partner's retirement priorities. Reach some agreement, even if it requires compromise.
- Don't guess. Know the income you need to lead the life you want to lead in retirement.
- When it comes to maintaining your health, there is no substitute for a good night's sleep.
- Don't let your assets be seriously compromised by legal entanglements and catastrophic health events.
- Anyone who retired prior to the age of Medicare eligibility faces the "gap years," when they may face higher healthcare premiums. It's important to consider your options for how you will pay for insurance during this time period.
- Consider using a Health Savings Account (HSA) as a method of bridging the time until Medicare eligibility.
- Ohio state law does not require public pensions to provide healthcare, and the rules for all plans are in a state of flux. Reductions in benefits or increases in costs are the current trend.

19

EXTRA SAVINGS
IN RETIREMENT

We don't like to dwell on it, but it's a fact—retirement means getting old, plus all the physical and financial challenges that come along with that. But, as the song goes, there is a silver lining behind every cloud.

This chapter summarizes a number of potential places you might find extra money. The trick is to have proper estimates and to make the right decisions with regard to those possibilities.

For example, without the need for uniform or proper work attire, the necessary clothing budget will likely be lowered. Being home may mean more time for cooking and eating at home, which means less money spent on expensive convenience foods or meals in restaurants. Without a daily commute, transportation costs may be lowered. In 2018, the Bureau of Labor Statistics (BLS) reported that in *the period just before retirement*, ages 55 to 64, the average annual expenditures of most workers totaled $66,212. The study also measured the costs of retirees between the ages of 65 to 74 and discovered their annual outlays were only $56,268. If you're doing the math, that's $9,944 less after retirement, which is more than $829 in savings every month. Where did these savings come from?[91]

The Housing Decision

The BLS survey found the cost of housing declines from an average of $20,907 for the group aged 55 to 64 to $18,007 for those between 65 to 74 years of age. At first, this may seem surprising, but it makes sense when you think about it, retirees often pay off their mortgage or downsize.

Food Costs: Up Or Down?

Generally, most people don't expect lower food costs in retirement. You may not eat less in retirement, but the time-saving though more expensive options, such as restaurants or ready-to-eat microwavable meals, are chosen less frequently.

According to the Bureau of Labor Statistics government report, those just before retirement had an average annual food expenditure of $7,923, up 2.5 percent from 2017, while those post-retirement baby boomers spent $7,164 during the year 2015 through 2016. As an added bonus, eating at home may even help any health goals you're working toward. The savings on food is significant in more ways than one.

Daily Travel

Avoiding a commute to work is among the most significant ways retirees save money. Dual-car families may even get rid of one car. The cost of daily travel is found to decline incrementally with age. For those in the age range of 55 to 64, the BLS survey calculated the mean travel costs at an annual average of $10,444 for 2018; this includes vehicle purchases, maintenance and repairs, insurance, gasoline, and motor oil. For retirees in their late 60s, that annual mean cost dropped to $7,270. And as people passed their 75th birthday, the cost of transportation averaged as little as $5,098 per year.[92]

Household Goods

Retirees also experience a reduced need for expensive consumer goods. Household appliances tend to be replaced less often, and furniture, too, is replaced less frequently. Your personal list and any associated savings will look different, but most don't consider how quickly these items add up or, in this case, subtract down.

Retirement Contributions

There is one more work-life budget expense that is always forgotten, and this one will certainly go away when you retire. It's the most obvious savings, too, although it's also commonly overlooked. When people leave their job to retire, *they no longer have to save money for retirement.* They stop contributing to a 401(k) or an individual retirement account, and they no longer contribute to pension accounts or Social Security.

According to the BLS study, the overall contributions to a long-term savings account drop from an average of $7,200 annually for people nearing retirement to just $2,800 annually among those ages 65 to 74. And since these numbers are readily available on your bank and investment statements, they should be easy for you to calculate into your retirement plan.

SUMMARY: Chapter 19

- Being retired might mean saving money on housing costs, food expenditures, commute-related expenses, and more.
- A big one: Retirement means you're no longer contributing to your retirement fund.

SECTION 5

THE CASE
FOR A FINANCIAL
QUARTERBACK

20

WHO'S IN CHARGE
OF YOUR TEAM?

T he goal of this book is to provide you with valuable information
in a highly digestible manner, information that you can actually
use as you continue to build a worry-free retirement plan. And,
as you are now aware, there is no one right way. Retirement plans are
not one-size-fits-all. A well-thought-out retirement plan should incor-
porate legal considerations, tax implications, and asset maximization for
beneficiaries that have been properly coordinated. And the best-of-
the-best plans are those specifically tailored to your situation, now and
in the future.

If you have invested wisely over the years, you probably have a group
of professional advisors that you call upon from time-to-time to handle
your various financial needs, including stockbrokers, life insurance
agents, property casualty agents, accountants, and attorneys. That's
great! And while every member of your team of professionals may be
well meaning, you need to ask yourself this question: Does your team
have an experienced leader who can work with your other specialists to
make sure that what needs to be accomplished on your behalf is executed professionally and cost effectively? And, equally importantly, does

that leader dot their i's and cross their t's to ensure that tens of thousands of dollars aren't left on the table because of a lack of coordination?

At this point, you have two choices. The first is to become a team leader yourself. Financial professionals call them "do-it-yourselfers." If you are inclined to be a do-it-yourselfer, that's fine. Just remember that you are now the quarterback of your entire financial plan. It's your job to call the right plays at the right time, and to make sure everybody is organized and optimized.

An important part of your job as team leader is to make sure you have all the latest information at hand to ensure your advisors are entirely independent, professionally unbiased, and do not benefit any more or less with whatever advice was given. Not everyone plays on the straight and narrow. It should come as no surprise that I have heard of lawyers charging to set up trusts that provided no extra protection, insurance agents who kept people in policies that outlived their intent, and, yes, even investment professionals who may not have had the most appropriate skill set for a particular job, but they took the job anyway because they did not want to turn a client away.

During the last 27 years, we've noticed that, try as they might, many do-it-yourselfers fall short of their needs and opportunities. Why? Primarily because the well-meaning professionals they employ tend to be loosely disconnected; they work for you, but they don't usually operate in coordination with one another. Put another way, you have a talented team of individual players and a detailed playbook, but the team leader just lacks the necessary experience.

Your financial plan is probably the most important thing you've ever created outside of your family, of course, so it had better be done right. At the risk of seeming self-serving, we strongly recommend having your plan "quarterbacked" by a knowledgeable professional, and having that plan reviewed for changes annually or anytime a meaningful life event occurs.

How To Identify A Financial Quarterback

It is not unrealistic to believe you have or will eventually accumulate $500,000 or more in retirement assets. Understanding how the affluent manage their wealth can provide anyone with useful insights. Almost always, they employ an Investment Advisor Representative to act as their Fiduciary. Some Investment Advisor Representatives may carry other professional designations, like Certified Financial Planner (CFP)[93] or Chartered Financial Analyst (CFA).[94]

Typically, the Investment Advisor Representative has discretion over your account, meaning they will actively trade your account in a manner that matches your goals and risk tolerance. Being a Fiduciary means they are always putting your best interests first; those who are CFPs and CFAs have gone through rigorous training and education, plus several years of experience, in order to master their fields.

Of the 271,900 so-called "personal financial advisors" in the industry as of 2016 (the latest year available from the Bureau of Labor Statistics), only about 28 percent are CFPs, and a mere 1.7 percent are CFAs. Why do so few professionals have designations? Because those designations are not easy to obtain; it takes years of study to fully understand this complex material and be able to pass the rigorous testing. Professionals are also required to have several years of industry experience in order to get that designation.

The majority of financial professionals you will meet have what are called standard industry licenses. But the problem with many industry licenses in any industry, not just financial services, is that they don't always equate to significant experience working with clients in a variety of situations. You need a well-certified, properly licensed professional with a great deal of experience who can help you coordinate all your various financial assets and advisors.

We believe you need a Financial Quarterback with the knowledge and expertise required to design and maintain custom portfolios and to do strategic financial planning that incorporates financial, tax, legal, and insurance solutions with full coordination.

Let's look at it another way. Would you ever get your heart operated on by anyone that is not a board-certified cardiologist? Have eye surgery by anyone other than an ophthalmologist? Have your foot operated on by anyone other than a podiatrist? Then why would you let anyone manage your hard-earned money if they haven't taken the time to become a true specialist in their field?

Responsibilities Of A Financial Quarterback

Your Financial Quarterback can help you calculate the potential costs of retirement while you're still working, and help you figure out which expenses can be reduced or eliminated entirely. Most people are usually pretty good at understanding their projected amount of resources and how income would change, but they often don't consider that the *need* for these resources would also shift either up or down in retirement. Including that consideration in the planning process is vital. Ideally, your plan should be reviewed for changes annually, or if a meaningful life event occurs.

For example, let's say a person decides they need to take money out of one of their accounts to pay for something outside of normal monthly expenses. They may decide to pull from a qualified account like an IRA, as opposed to a non-qualified account where the taxes may be lower. As a result, they may suddenly incur taxes on their Social Security benefits, and their Medicare premiums may become higher.

One uncoordinated decision can have a ripple effect, with the result being that you might net a lot less in retirement than you could have. This is the equivalent of burning money or, to utilize our running football analogy, losing yards. You may have the best receivers on your team, but if they're standing someplace other than where the ball was being passed, they are going to be less successful. That's where the Quarterback comes in. Placing a knowledgeable professional at the head of a team of others who are great at what they do can help to reduce wasted money and to protect your assets in a well-thought-out, perfectly executed way.

Another invaluable benefit of having an experienced Financial Quarterback is that they will build an atmosphere of trust among all your team members so that everybody is willing to go the extra mile for one another. If I were to call the accountant and let them know I have something critically important that needs to be evaluated in the next 24 hours, the accountant will act in a way that helps the rest of the team; they are going to better serve the client. As a result, it elevates the entire team and their productivity.

Barriers To Seeking Professional Advice

Why do so many people insist they can do it all themselves? There are two main reasons.

The First Reason: Cost. A lot of people think that only the very wealthy can afford an integrated and coordinated estate plan. That is incorrect. There are a number of practical steps that YOU can take now to save your heirs time and money later. For example, stretch IRAs can help avoid probate costs and complexity. You should make sure all your retirement payouts take full advantage of such provisions.

The Second Reason: Most people simply don't know what they don't know. They don't know which topics to research and which questions to ask. And that can lead to costly mistakes, because it simply isn't easy to properly coordinate all the areas in your financial life. Let's look at an example.

I enjoy holding panel discussion and educational workshops throughout Northeastern Ohio. As part of these events, I invite many of the financial "players" who provide coordinated support for my clients. It's not uncommon for an audience question to be answered by multiple members of the team, and the audience is always impressed. Perhaps the insurance expert starts off answering, and then he hands it off to the lawyer, who carries the answer for a while before handing it back to the insurance expert to add more. Then the investment professional takes over for a time, and then the accountant finishes things off.

When a team has played together for a few seasons, each player knows what the others are doing, which enables them to provide service much quicker and more efficiently than if someone tries to guess what the other is thinking. When I talk to attendees who opt for subsequent meetings in my office, they almost always have the same observation: "I learned a lot more than I imagined."

I also learn from a high percentage of these attendees that I'm just one address on a long list of professionals to meet with. They may have visited with an attorney to talk about estate planning. Or they may have met with their life insurance representative to see if they can take the cash benefit out of a policy, thinking they no longer feel the need for that protection. Or they may have met with any of a host of other related professionals who are likely to provide just one small piece to the retirement planning puzzle and leave it to the client to figure out the best plan overall.

An experienced, reputable Financial Quarterback only wants to see you moving down the field as swiftly and easily as rules and conditions allow. Whether that means coordinating with the accountant or attorney for tax planning and wills, advising you on the proper asset allocation, providing advice on taking a lump sum, or taking the right survivorship pension option for your situation, a solid Financial Quarterback will connect you with the right players to make the best play. Seeing the right person will help you save time and avoid confusion, not to mention the messy process of learning by making mistakes. And your Financial Quarterback sees the whole field; they will tell you exactly what strategies to implement to help get you to the end zone.

That's how most of my clients view me—just as important to their finances as their primary care physician is to their health, and the one they see first for all things financial, even when they know they are going to be referred to a specialist.

Finding The Right Quarterback

In football, before a professional team drafts or trades for a player, they make sure the player fits their needs; they have to have the right qualifications and skills for the task at hand.

You should do the same thing when it comes time to "draft" your financial quarterback. There are a lot of important things to consider. Here are a few questions you might want to ask:

1. What qualifications, degrees, and designations does your Financial Quarterback have, such as CFP®, CFA®, CPA, etc?
2. How long has the firm been in business?
3. How many clients do they have?
4. How does their professional advisor coordination work?
5. Is the firm a complete organization or a one-to-three-person shop?

Remember: Next to raising a family, the financial decisions you make in life are probably the most important challenges you'll face. So take the time to find people you trust that are good listeners, have the proper resources, and have a proven track record, preferably with Ohio public service employees.

You may have to interview many financial advisors to find the best central figure, the best Financial Quarterback for you, but they can more than cover their cost in time, money, and other headaches.

SUMMARY: Chapter 20

- Successful, worry-free retirement plans will require regular oversight to capitalize on opportunities and protect your wealth from impending risk.
- Do-it-yourselfers with $500,000 or more in retirement assets usually discover the dollars saved in fees was not worth the risk to their financial and emotional well-being.
- Make sure you have the right people managing, growing, and protecting your retirement assets. Look for designations such as CFP along with a proven track record.
- Using an experienced Financial Quarterback does not guarantee investment success, but it certainly helps your chances!

21

LITTLE THINGS
MEAN A LOT

want to thank you for taking the time to read this book. I hope it has
been informative, enjoyable, and easy to understand. This final chapter is different than most financial books.

A few years ago, I read a book entitled *The Compound Effect* written
by a well-respected life coach, Darren Hardy.[95] The book has a life-
altering proposition. Make small, smart choices, consistently over time,
and you will see a radical difference in your quality of life or anything
that you put your mind to.

For the past several years, I've applied Darren's principles to my own
life. They worked. I learned how wonderful and fulfilling my life is
NOW, and how it will be even more so in the FUTURE. It is in that
spirit that I offer some important lessons I have learned as I applied *The
Compound Effect* to my own life. My hope is that they will make your
life more wonderful NOW and in the FUTURE.

•   •   •

Lesson #1: Own A Positive Mental Attitude

Great things don't usually happen overnight. Accomplishing something important usually takes time, dedication, practice, and a commitment to steady progress over time. I have found over the years that some people resent others for their success or feel others are luckier than they are. Is it really luck? Or could it be that others have taken the preparation and hard work behind the scenes that was necessary to get ahead in their lives?

Many times, this resentment leads to a more negative outlook. When someone isn't taking the time to increase their education or job skills, they may let their emotions cloud their judgment and decision making. This pessimistic life view will impact everything in your life, including your health as well as your wealth. One of the best ways to exude positive energy every day is to live by some simple basic fundamentals, ones that are important to you, and apply the virtue of persistence.

Lesson #2: Don't Let Your Emotions Cloud Your Judgment

Many people do this with their financial portfolios; they let current events and the mob mentalities affect their decision making. When people chase whatever seems "hot," like buying bitcoins in 2018, or selling things when the markets are low and it seems like everything is doom and gloom, there can be long-term negative consequences.

These types of individuals also have a tendency to buy high *after* huge profits have been made in whatever stock is the flavor of the month, because they feel like they are going to miss out if they don't jump on the bandwagon. All too often, this kind of impulsive decision is not wise.

Lesson #3: Periodically Recharge Your Batteries

Take the time to rejuvenate and recharge your internal batteries. For me, this might be a day where I don't watch CNBC, when I don't even pick up financial magazines, or otherwise let my mind dwell on other, non-work things. For me to *really* recharge my batteries, I have found the best way is to be by water. That's why we own a lake house on Chautauqua Lake in upstate New York.

When I first bought that house, I needed to rent it out for part of the year to defray some of the costs of upkeep and maintenance. We had wanted to find a place within a 2 1/2–hour drive from home, and to find a place where we could spend quality time with our children and make great memories together. We've been very fortunate; we no longer rent the property, and the family has a wonderful bank of memories built already, with more to come.

But that's just me. Now is the time to think about *you*. How do you relax? What's the best way for you to really recharge your own batteries?

Lesson #4: Find Something Else You Love To Do

Have a hobby or something you love to do that helps you escape your normal stresses in your life. My clients enjoy a wide range of personal hobbies, such as woodworking, rebuilding classic cars, flying airplanes and helicopters, hunting, knitting, scrapbooking, and much more. I personally enjoy sports like snow skiing, water skiing, boating, sailing, golfing, and hunting. Get me outdoors and I'm happy!

It's not enough to just relax; you need to find ways to keep busy, activities that challenge your mind and keep you engaged in something larger. Find something that you are passionate about and give it a try. It might just be what the doctor ordered.

Lesson #5: Pay Yourself First

We all have excuses why we cannot save more money. In order to have a truly worry-free retirement, we need to have no excuses. You don't want to find yourself looking at your financial assets when you're 70 and saying, "If only I had. . . ."

So here are two starter suggestions. First off, put aside 15 to 20 percent of your gross pay. Invest it in some way and put it to work for your future. Second, take half of every raise you get and put that away. Reward yourself with half of the raise—you earned it, after all—and save the other half, preferably in a pre-tax vehicle such as a 457, 403(b), or 401(k).

Lesson #6: Take Time To Smell The Roses

Be grateful for the progress you have made thus far. If you aren't happy with your personal progress, don't frown on the past; focus instead on how to change the future. Dwelling on the past won't get you anywhere. Doing something about it is the only reasonable course of action.

Lesson #7: Stay Humble And Learn From Others

Learn from the progress and the mistakes of others. You don't have to reinvent the wheel or get your shins kicked in all the time. Chances are there are people out there that have already made similar mistakes and overcame them. Learn from others, and when you do make mistakes, learn from them so you don't repeat them.

Lesson #8: Take Care Of The Ones You Love

Life is about balance. This is true with how you work, how you sleep, and how you play; it's also true with your wealth. It's essential to make sure you and your loved ones are always properly taken care of. That means having all your insurances (life, disability, health, property, and casualty, etc.) set up with proper coverage and limits. It means designating beneficiaries, and updating those designations as necessary. It means putting money away for your children's education, your own retirement, that vacation you've long dreamed of, and even a second home, if you so desire.

And, when it comes to your investments, don't have all your eggs in one basket. Make sure your portfolio is properly diversified and your risk is balanced.

Lesson #9: Use Debt Intelligently

Debt is not a bad thing if you have the right kind. Debt can actually be used to your advantage, assuming you don't get carried away with it and let it take over your finances.

Some debts can help you obtain some of the necessities in life, especially when you are just starting out and you're thinking of buying your first home or your first car. Debt can also be used to buy a rental property, which will ultimately build your wealth by letting others pay off the debt and possibly picking up some tax deductions along the way.

Lesson #10: Pay Only Your Fair Share Of Taxes

I'm all for paying my fair share. But like most people, I don't want to pay a dime more than I have to. It's far too common for people already in retirement to take money out of their taxable IRAs and reinvest their interest, dividends, and capital gains, all of which are also taxable each year. These people end up paying a lot more tax than they have to.

There are lots and lots of solid tax strategies out there. The trick is to identify the best ones for your particular situation, and then monitor and keep abreast of changes as time goes by. Take nothing for granted.

Lesson #11: Integrate New Life Habits

Have you ever heard of the 21-day rule? When you're trying to develop a new habit, one trick is to consciously do it every day for 21 days. Before you know it, you've got a new habit. If you don't believe me, try it for yourself.

Lesson #12: Work-Life Balance: Plan Your Days Appropriately

I didn't invent this system; it comes from Dan Sullivan and his Strategic Coach program,[96] and it has been a major game changer in my business and personal life. Here's the breakdown: Free Days, Focus Days, and Buffer Days.

- Free Day: Twenty-four hours of doing nothing work related. These days are used to rejuvenate you and to do some things that really make your happy (see Lesson #3).
- Focus Day: Concentrate on your unique abilities (the things you do best).
- Buffer Day: Use these days to clean up the clutter in your life and work habits, so that you can have better Free and Focus Days.

Lesson #13: Surround Yourself With Great People

I know there are a lot of people in the world who are much smarter than I am. My experience is that many of them are willing to help you on your journey if you just take the time to ask.

This applies to hobbies, passions, careers, family life, and most importantly, maintaining a positive mental attitude. Surround yourself with people with a wide range of life experience and learn from them.

Lesson #14: Always Say Thank You

Saying *thank you* doesn't cost a penny. Yet so few people see the value in being thankful for the things we have every day, or don't think it's necessary to acknowledge that gratitude openly. That applies to friends, families, associates, and advisors.

In my case, it also applies to you, the reader. I want to thank you for taking the time to read this book. I hope it has provided some information you can use in an understandable manner.

One final comment to civil service workers, to whom this book was dedicated to helping. The Lineweaver family (at home and in the office) wants to thank you, for everything you do for us every day. You make sure we have a WONDERFUL and SAFE LIFE. Our thanks go out to you.

Nothing provided herein constitutes tax advice. Individuals should seek the advice of their own tax advisor for specific information regarding tax consequences of investments. Investments in securities entail risk and are not suitable for all investors. This is not a recommendation or an offer to sell (or a solicitation of an offer to buy) securities in the United States or any other jurisdiction. In the real-life scenarios and other stories throughout the book, names have been changed and stories have been altered to protect clients' identities and simplified for clarity. Some stories are hypothetical, and are for illustrative purposes only.

ENDNOTES

1. **John Martin Richardson, Jr. (Born March 12, 1938):** Is an American academic who writes, lectures, and consults in applied systems analysis, international development, conflict-development linkages, and the sustainability and resilience of political-economic-social institutions. He currently serves as Visiting Professor at the Lee Kuan Yew School of Public Policy and Director of Outreach and Projects at Residential College 4 at the National University of Singapore.
https://infogalactic.com/info/John_M._Richardson_(professor)

2. **Dow Jones Industrial Average, December 17, 2018:** Stock Market News, Wall Street collapsed on Friday following investors' concerns of an impending global economic slowdown. A series of weaker-than-expected economic reports from China and European Union raised eyebrows of several market participants. All three major stock indexes closed in the red. For the week also, these indexes ended in negative territory. The Dow Jones Industrial Average (DJI) closed at 24,100.51, plunging 2 percent or 496.87 points.
https://www.nasdaq.com/articles/stock-market-news-dec-17-2018-2018-12-17

3. **Moody's Investors Service:** Often referred to as Moody's, is the bond credit rating business of Moody's Corporation, representing the company's traditional line of business and its historical name. Moody's Investors Service provides international financial research on bonds issued by commercial and government entities. Moody's, along with Standard & Poor's and Fitch Group, is considered one of the Big Three credit rating agencies. The company ranks the creditworthiness of borrowers using a standardized ratings scale which measures expected investor loss in the event of default.
https://en.wikipedia.org/wiki/Moody%27s_Investors_Service

4. **The State Pension Funding Gap, 2017 PEW:** Funding gap in 2017 shows economic recovery has not lowered debt: States reported a total liability of $4.1 trillion in pension obligations to workers and retirees in 2017, and $2.9 trillion in assets set aside to pay for those benefits, creating the funding gap of $1.28 trillion. This was a decrease from the previous year's gap of $1.35 trillion and only the second reported decrease since the recession. Overall in 2017, states had 69 percent of the assets they needed to fully fund their pension liabilities—ranging from 34 percent in Kentucky to 103 percent in Wisconsin. In addition to Kentucky, four other states—Colorado, Connecticut, Illinois, and New Jersey—were less than 50 percent funded, and another 15 had less than two-thirds of the assets they needed to pay their pension obli-

gations. Only Idaho, Nebraska, New York, North Carolina, South Dakota, Tennessee, and Utah joined Wisconsin in being at least 90 percent funded (Figure 1). https://www.pewtrusts.org/en/research-and-analysis/issue-briefs/2019/06/the-state-pension-funding-gap-2017

5. **Multiemployer Pension Reform Act Of 2014:** Was enacted on December 16, 2014. In the new law, Congress established new options for trustees of multiemployer plans that will potentially run out of money. Under MPRA, plan trustees of multiemployer plans can submit an application to the Treasury Department showing that proposed pension benefit reductions are necessary to keep a plan from running out of money.
https://www.pbgc.gov/prac/multiemployer/multiemployer-pension-reform-act-of-2014

6. **Iron Workers Union Of Cleveland Ohio:** Iron Workers pension cuts approved; retirees to get smaller checks. Workers atop what was to become the SOHIO headquarters, later BP Tower, in downtown Cleveland. In a vote pitting current workers against retirees, their union has agreed to cut pension payments.
https://www.cleveland.com/nation/2017/01/iron_workers_pension_cuts_are.html

7. **Sears Holdings:** Sears owner gets $250 million lifeline, says it will shut 96 more stores—Here's where they are Published Thu, Nov 7 2019 3:36 PM EST Updated Fri, Nov 8 2019 9:37 AM EST Lauren Thomas. As the holiday season approaches, the parent company of Sears and Kmart has secured a $250 million lifeline and announced plans on Thursday to shut 96 more stores. That will leave the business with 182 locations. The financing came from lenders that include owner Eddie Lampert. Transformco added it is taking the steps to focus on its "competitive strengths." But it faces "a difficult retail environment and other challenges." When Lampert bought Sears out of bankruptcy court for $5.2 billion earlier this year, he acquired 425 Sears and Kmart locations. He argued at the time that his offer was the best option to keep stores open and save thousands of jobs.
https://www.cnbc.com/2019/11/07/sears-owner-gets-250-million-lifeline-says-it-will-shut-another-96-stores.html

8. **Deferred Compensation Plans:** Is a type of nonqualified, tax advantaged deferred-compensation retirement plan that is available for governmental and certain nongovernmental employers in the United States. The employer provides the plan and the employee defers compensation into it on a pre-tax or after-tax (Roth) basis. For the most part, the plan operates similarly to a 401(k) or 403(b) plan with which most people in the US are familiar. The key difference is that unlike with a 401(k) plan, it has no 10 percent penalty for withdrawal before the age of 55 (59 for IRA accounts) (although the withdrawal is subject to ordinary income taxation). These 457 plans (both governmental and nongovernmental) can also allow independent contractors to participate in the plan, where 401(k) and 403(b) plans cannot.
https://en.wikipedia.org/wiki/457_plan

9. **American Express Company:** Also known as Amex, is an American multinational financial services corporation headquartered in Three World Financial Center in New York City. The company was founded in 1850 and is one of the 30 components

of the Dow Jones Industrial Average. The company is best known for its charge card, credit card, and traveler's cheque businesses.
https://en.wikipedia.org/wiki/American_Express.

Public Sector Pension Plans: The first corporate pension in the U.S. was established by the American Express Company in 1875. Prior to that, most companies were small or family-run businesses. The plan applied to workers who had been with the company for 20 years of service, had reached age 60 and had been recommended for retirement by a manager and approved by a committee along with the board of directors. Workers who made it received half of their annual salary in retirement, up to a maximum of $500, according to the Bureau of Labor Statistics.
https://www.thebalance.com the-history-of-the-pension-plan-2894374

10. **LinkedIn:** Is an American business and employment-oriented service that operates via websites and mobile apps. Founded on December 28, 2002, and launched on May 5, 2003, it is mainly used for professional networking, including employers posting jobs and job seekers posting their CVs. As of 2015, most of the company's revenue came from selling access to information about its members to recruiters and sales professionals. Since December 2016 it has been a wholly owned subsidiary of Microsoft.
https://en.wikipedia.org/wiki/LinkedIn

11. **401(k):** In the United States, a 401(k) plan is the tax-qualified, defined-contribution pension account defined in subsection 401(k) of the Internal Revenue Code. Under the plan, retirement savings contributions are provided (and sometimes proportionately matched) by an employer, deducted from the employee's paycheck before taxation (therefore tax deferred until withdrawn after retirement or as otherwise permitted by applicable law), and limited to a maximum pre-tax annual contribution of $19,500 (as of 2020). https://en.wikipedia.org/wiki/401(k)

    403(b): In the United States, a 403(b) plan is a U.S. tax-advantaged retirement savings plan available for public education organizations, some non-profit employers (only Internal Revenue Code 501(c)(3) organizations), cooperative hospital service organizations, and self-employed ministers in the United States. It has tax treatment similar to a 401(k) plan, especially after the Economic Growth and Tax Relief Reconciliation Act of 2001.
https://en.wikipedia.org/wiki/403(b)

12. **Mayor Rawlings Warns Of "Fan Blades That Look Like Bankruptcy" Over Police And Fire Pension:** Dallas Mayor Mike Rawlings sat in front of the Texas State Pension Review Board Thursday morning, arguing, he believed, for his city's continued existence. "It is horribly ironic that a city that has enjoyed such tremendous success, a city that has made Texas so strong and so proud is potentially walking into the fan blades that look like bankruptcy," Rawlings said. "Shame on me, shame on you, shame on all of us if we allow that to happen." The specter haunting Rawlings is the Dallas Police and Fire Pension System's multi-billion dollar unfunded liability, which, should it go unaddressed, could leave the pension fund bankrupt by 2030.
https://www.dallasobserver.com/news/mayor-rawlings-warns-of-fan-blades-that -look-like-bankruptcy-over-police-and-fire-pension-8873598

    Dallas, Texas 2019: A new analysis of the latest available audited financial report found Dallas has a Taxpayer Burden™ of $21,600, earning it an "F" grade based on

Truth in Accounting's grading scale. Dallas' elected officials have made repeated financial decisions that have left the city with a debt burden of $7.8 billion, according to the analysis. That equates to a $21,600 burden for every city taxpayer. Dallas' financial problems stem mostly from unfunded retirement obligations that have accumulated over many years. Of the $13.3 billion in retirement benefits promised, the city has not funded $7.3 billion in pension and $499.9 million in retiree healthcare benefits. Page 82.
https://www.truthinaccounting.org/library/doclib/2019-Financial-State-of-the
-Cities-Report—1.pdf

13. ***Hidden Debt, Hidden Deficits—2017 Edition: How Pension Promises Are Consuming State And Local Budgets* By Joshua D. Rauh:** The unfunded obligations of the pension systems sponsored by state and local governments in the United States continue to grow. In this second annual report on the off-balance-sheet pension promises of state and local governments, we study in detail 649 pension systems around the United States, including all of the main pension systems of the states, the largest U.S. cities, and the largest U.S. counties. We report on both their own measurements of their costs and obligations, and how these differ from market valuations that are consistent with the principles of financial economics.
https://www.hoover.org/sites/default/files/research/docs/rauh_hiddendebt2017
_final_webreadypdf1.pdf

14. **Hoover Institution:** With its eminent scholars and world-renowned Library and Archives, the Hoover Institution seeks to improve the human condition by advancing ideas that promote economic opportunity and prosperity, while securing and safeguarding peace for America and all mankind.
https://www.hoover.org/about

15. **Ohio State Teachers Retirement System (STRS):** State Teachers Retirement System of Ohio is one of the nation's premier retirement systems, serving nearly 494,000 active, inactive and retired Ohio public educators. With investment assets of $79.9 billion (including short-term investments) as of June 30, 2018, STRS Ohio is one of the largest public pension funds in the country.
https://www.strsoh.org/aboutus/
State Employees Retirement System (SERS): Protecting and growing the retirement contributions of our members and their employers is our priority. In fiscal year 2018, SERS served 158,343 active, contributing members and 81,332 benefit recipients. SERS paid out over $1.3 billion in pension and healthcare reimbursements of which more than $1.2 billion was returned to Ohio's economy.
https://www.ohsers.org/about-sers/
Police & Fire Pension Fund (OP&F): OP&F was created in 1965 by the Ohio General Assembly to provide pension and disability benefits to the state's full-time police officers and firefighters. OP&F also provides survivor benefits and offers an optional healthcare plan for retirees and their eligible dependents. Operations began in 1967, when assets of $75 million and liabilities of $490 million were transferred from 454 local public safety pension funds across Ohio. As of spring 2018, OP&F's investment portfolio was valued at $15.7 billion.
https://www.ohprs.org/ohprs/about.jsp

Highway Patrol Retirement System (HPRS): In 1941, the Ohio General Assembly established the Highway Patrol Retirement System (HPRS) for troopers and communications personnel employed by the Highway Patrol. Today, membership in HPRS is limited to troopers with arrest authority and trooper cadets in training at the Highway Patrol Training Academy. The system provides age and service, disability, survivor, and death benefits, as well as healthcare coverage for benefit recipients and eligible dependents. As of March 31, 2019, HPRS had estimated assets of $880 million.
https://www.ohprs.org/ohprs/about.jsp

Ohio Public Employees Retirement System (OPERS): Since 1935, the Ohio Public Employees Retirement System (OPERS) has meant security and peace of mind to millions of Ohio's retired public workers and their families. With unaudited defined benefit and healthcare investment assets of $101.4 billion as of Dec. 31, 2017.
https://www.opers.org/about/

16. **Ohio State Assembly:** How to find your House Representative.
https://www.legislature.ohio.gov/

17. **Ohio Senator Tom Niehaus:** Is the former President of the Ohio Senate. He served from 2011 to 2012. He also was the state senator for the 14th District from 2005 to 2012. He served in the Ohio House of Representatives from 2001 to 2004.
https://en.wikipedia.org/wiki/Tom_Niehaus

18. **John Richard Kasich Jr. (Born May 13, 1952):** Is an American politician, author, and television news host who served as the 69th Governor of Ohio from 2011 to 2019. Kasich is a Republican.
https://en.wikipedia.org/wiki/John_Kasich

19. **William G. Batchelder III (Born December 19, 1942):** Was the 101st Speaker of the Ohio House of Representatives, serving from 2011 to 2014. He also represented the 69th District of the Ohio House of Representatives from 2007 to 2014, and served in the House from 1969 to 1998 previously.
https://en.wikipedia.org/wiki/William_G._Batchelder

20. **Abramowicz, Lisa, "5% Is The New 8% For Pension Funds:"** For years, many pension funds assumed they would earn an average 8 percent annually from their investments. Bloomberg Businessweek, August 2, 2017.
https://www.bloomberg.com/news/articles/2017-08-02/5-is-the-new-8-for-reliable-returns-for-pension-funds

21. **United States Pensions Funds:** Retirement Assets Top $29 Trillion, While Plan Fees Continue Downward Trend By Ted Godbout June 27, 2019. Industry Trends and Research .Since the end of last year, total U.S. retirement assets were up 7.4%, reaching $29.1 trillion at the end of the first quarter for 2019, according to new data by the Investment Company Institute.
https://www.napa-net.org/news-info/daily-news/retirement-assets-top-29-trillion-while-plan-fees-continue-downward-trend

22. **Cost-Of-Living Adjustment (COLA) Information For 2020:** Social Security and Supplemental Security Income (SSI) benefits for nearly 69 million Americans will increase 1.6 percent in 2020. The 1.6 percent cost-of-living adjustment (COLA)

will begin with benefits payable to more than 63 million Social Security beneficiaries in January 2020. Increased payments to more than 8 million SSI beneficiaries will begin on December 31, 2019. (Note: some people receive both Social Security and SSI benefits).
https://www.ssa.gov/cola/

23. **Erick M. Elder:** Joined the University of Arkansas at Little Rock in 1996. His areas of specialization are statistics, macroeconomics, international economics, and public finance. Elder is also a policy advisor for The Heartland Institute.
https://www.heartland.org/about-us/who-we-are/erick-m-elder

24. **Dr. David Mitchell:** Is the Director of the Arkansas Center for Research in Economics. He earned his BA and MA in economics from Clemson University and was awarded his PhD from George Mason University. While at George Mason, he had the pleasure of studying under two Nobel laureates: James Buchanan and Vernon Smith. Prior to earning his PhD, he worked in the insurance industry in both the United States and Germany.
https://uca.edu/acre/our-people/

25. ***Ohio Public Pension System—Traditional Funding Ratios Are Not Enough For Pension Funds:*** Ohio's largest pension plans are at risk of falling significantly short on their obligations to hundreds of thousands of Ohioans. In fact, Ohio ranks ahead of only Mississippi in terms of the level of unfunded liabilities relative to the size of the state's income. Despite having assets of more than $150 billion, some estimates show that Ohio needs to increase pension funding by at least $275 billion to be fully funded—that's almost $25,000 per Ohio citizen.
www.mercatus.org/ohiopensions

26. **Ohio Public Pension System:** Traditional Funding Ratios Are Not Enough For Pension Funds: Ohio's public pension system comprises five state-level plans that have actuarial funding ratios ranging between 67 and 84 percent. Pension plan funding levels are a proxy for the ability of a pension plan to fund its promised benefit payments without additional resources.
https://papers.ssrn.com/sol3/papers.cfm?abstract_id=3191486

27. **Ohio Public Pension System:** Traditional Funding Ratios Are Not Enough for Pension Funds: State Budget Solutions report on the nation's public pension plans warns that most are severely underfunded, and Ohio's five state-level public pension plans are not exceptions. Ohio ranks behind only Mississippi in terms of its level of unfunded liabilities relative to the size of the state's income.
https://www.mercatus.org/system/files/mercatus-elder-ohio-public-pension-v2.pdf
Ohio's Public Pension Systems Lost Money In 2018, Returns Show: COLUMBUS — Each of Ohio's five public pension systems, which serve nearly 1.9 million workers, retirees and beneficiaries, lost money on their investment portfolios in 2018, putting more pressure on the retirement systems.
https://www.daytondailynews.com/news/ohio-public-pension-systems-lost-money-2018-returns-show/NucbE3AFUSMwDNvORIvLIJ/

28. **UNACCOUNTABLE AND UNAFFORDABLE December 2017:** Unfunded liabilities of public pension plans continue to loom over state governments nationwide. If net pension assets are determined using more realistic investment return assump-

tions, pension funding gaps are much wider than even the large sums reported in state financial documents. Unfunded liabilities (using a risk-free rate of return assumption) of state-administered pension plans now exceed $6 trillion—an increase of $433 billion since our 2016 report. The national average funding ratio is a mere 33.7 percent, amounting to $18,676 dollars of unfunded liabilities for every resident of the United States.
https://www.alec.org/app/uploads/2017/12/2017-Unaccountable-and-Unaffordable -FINAL_DEC_WEB.pdf

29. **Defining And Quantifying The Pension Liabilities Of Government Entities In The United States:** In 2016, Moody's Investors Service (Moody's) estimated that U.S. federal, state, and local government employee pension plans were underfunded by about $7 trillion, with $3.5 trillion (equal to approximately 20% of the U.S. gross domestic product [GDP]) coming from the underfunded defined benefit (DB) obligations of federal government employees (Bryan, 2016).
https://onlinelibrary.wiley.com/doi/full/10.1002/jcaf.22320
The Time Bomb Inside Public Pension Plans: Aug 23, 2018- Sanitation workers, firefighters, teachers and other state and local government employees have performed their duties in the public sector for decades with the understanding that their often lackluster salaries were propped up by excellent benefits, including an ironclad pension. But Moody's Investors Service recently estimated that public pensions are underfunded by $4.4 trillion. That amount, which is equivalent to the economy of Germany, accounts for one-fifth of national debt. It's a significant concern for public employees who were banking on a fully funded retirement to get them through their golden years.
https://knowledge.wharton.upenn.edu/article/the-time-bomb-inside-public -pension-plans/

30. **John J. Gallagher Fund Director Of OP&F Ohio:** Has been selected by the Ohio Police & Fire Pension Fund (OP&F) Board of Trustees as the retirement system's next executive director, effective Jan. 1, 2013. Staff, the Board of Trustees and its healthcare consultant continue to work toward a major transition in how OP&F will offer access to retiree healthcare coverage beginning in 2019. A search began during the summer for a firm to assist OP&F in the transition from a group-sponsored healthcare plan to a new consumer-driven model to be in place by Jan. 1, 2019. Three finalists emerged from the search during September. These finalists presented their ideas to the Board on Sept. 26 and 27. Once a firm is selected, work will begin on the new healthcare plan.
https://www.op-f.org/Files/membersreportfall2017.pdf

31. **New Data Analyzed By Truth In Accounting:** Reveal that Ohio public pensions are not being fully-funded. By Truth in Accounting, News Partner | May 10, 2017 2:26 pm ET | Updated May 10, 2017 2:33 pm ET.
https://patch.com/ohio/cincinnati/how-well-are-ohio-public-pensions-funded
OPEB: In total, debt among the states was $1.5 trillion at the end of the 2018 fiscal year.
https://www.truthinaccounting.org/library/doclib/FSOS-booklet-2019.pdf

32. **Truth In Accounting:** Formerly known as the Institute for Truth in Accounting, is a non-partisan American think tank and an associate of the State Policy Network. TIA's

stated goal is the promotion of transparent government financial information to citizens. TIA analyzes government finances on the city, state, and federal level. Each September, TIA releases its "Financial State of States" report that takes a deep look into each of the 50 states' Comprehensive Annual Financial Report (CAFR) in order to compare assets with liabilities. "For the first time, a detailed analysis of pension and healthcare liabilities has exposed all fifty states' actual obligations," commented Ziyi Mai in The John Locke Foundation's blog, The Locker Room. TIA then ranks the 50 states on the basis of taxpayer burden, which is each taxpayer's share of state debt. https://en.wikipedia.org/wiki/Truth_in_Accounting

33. **Ohio State:** Debt burden of $26.6 billion burden equates to $6,600 for every taxpayer in the state. taxpayer
https://www.truthinaccounting.org/library/doclib/FSOS-booklet-2019.pdf

34. **Michael William Krzyzewski:** Nicknamed "Coach K"; born February 13, 1947) is an American college basketball coach and former player. Since 1980, he has served as the head men's basketball coach at Duke University, where he has led the Blue Devils to five NCAA Championships, 12 Final Fours, 12 ACC regular season titles, and 15 ACC Tournament championships. Among men's college basketball coaches, only UCLA's John Wooden has won more NCAA Championships with a total of 10. Krzyzewski has the most wins of any coach in college basketball history.
https://en.wikipedia.org/wiki/Mike_Krzyzewski
Jay Bilas: Said Krzyzewski often saw NBA or college players taking the opportunity to travel the world as routine. Bilas said he would often say "don't take special for granted."
https://pilotonline.com/entertainment/article_c2adcae3-f392-5fa9-888b-b1cc06
b8f2b7.html

35. **ROTH Contributions:** A Roth IRA can be an individual retirement account containing investments in securities, usually common stocks and bonds, often through mutual funds (although other investments, including derivatives, notes, certificates of deposit, and real estate are possible). A Roth IRA can also be an individual retirement annuity, which is an annuity contract or an endowment contract purchased from a life insurance company. As with all IRAs, the Internal Revenue Service mandates specific eligibility and filing status requirements. A Roth IRA's main advantages are its tax structure and the additional flexibility that this tax structure provides. Also, there are fewer restrictions on the investments that can be made in the plan than many other tax-advantaged plans, and this adds somewhat to their popularity, though the investment options available depend on the trustee (or the place where the plan is established). 2019 age 49 and below $6,000, Age 50 and above $7,000. The Roth IRA was established by the Taxpayer Relief Act of 1997.
https://en.wikipedia.org/wiki/Roth_IRA

36. **Retirement Plan And IRA Required Minimum Distributions FAQs:** The Setting Every Community Up for Retirement Enhancement Act of 2019 (SECURE Act) became law on December 20, 2019. The Secure Act made major changes to the RMD rules. If you reached the age of 70 1/2 in 2019 the prior rule applies, and you must take your first RMD by April 1, 2020. If you reach age 70 1/2 in 2020 or later you must take your first RMD by April 1 of the year after you reach 72. For defined

contribution plan participants, or Individual Retirement Account (IRA) owners, who die after December 31, 2019, (with a delayed effective date for certain collectively bargained plans), the SECURE Act requires the entire balance of the participant's account be distributed within ten years. There is an exception for a surviving spouse, a child who has not reached the age of majority, a disabled or chronically ill person or a person not more than ten years younger than the employee or IRA account owner. The new 10-year rule applies regardless of whether the participant dies before, on, or after, the required beginning date, now age 72.
https://www.irs.gov/retirement-plans/retirement-plans-faqs-regarding-required-minimum-distributions

37. **About Publication 590-B, Distributions From Individual Retirement Arrangements (IRAs):** Publication 590-B discusses distributions from individual retirement arrangements (IRAs). An IRA is a personal savings plan that gives you tax advantages for setting aside money for retirement. For information about contributions to an IRA, see Publication 590-A, Contributions to Individual Retirement Arrangements (IRAs).
https://www.irs.gov/forms-pubs/about-publication-590-b

38. **OP&F Healthcare:** Ohio Police & Fire Pension Fund Healthcare Transition by, OPBA Attorney Brian Holb. As many of you are all too aware, the Ohio Police and Fire Pension Fund transitioned to providing retirees with a stipend to cover a portion of their healthcare costs. In early 2017, the OP&F Board of Trustees decided to re-structure the retiree healthcare plan. This restructuring ended the group-sponsored model. The new model went into effect on January 1, 2019. OP&F's stated reason for the change is to extend available funding for the healthcare plan for approximately 15 years. The OPBA has been watching this process closely and providing assistance to members when needed. OPBA leadership expressed their grave concerns about transitioning to a stipend model in early 2017 with Director. Unfortunately, the implementation of the stipend model has been worse than anyone anticipated.
https://www.opba.com/?zone=/unionactive/view_subarticle.cfm&subHomeID=127510&topHomeID=737046&page=NEWS

39. **Internal Revenue Code Section 1031:** Like-kind exchanges—when you exchange real property used for business or held as an investment solely for other business or investment property that is the same type or "like-kind"—have long been permitted under the Internal Revenue Code. Generally, if you make a like-kind exchange, you are not required to recognize a gain or loss under Internal Revenue Code Section 1031. If, as part of the exchange, you also receive other (not like-kind) property or money, you must recognize a gain to the extent of the other property and money received. You can't recognize a loss. Under the Tax Cuts and Jobs Act, Section 1031 now applies only to exchanges of real property and not to exchanges of personal or intangible property.
https://www.irs.gov/businesses/small-businesses-self-employed/like-kind-exchanges-real-estate-tax-tips

40. ***Starker Versus The United States:*** United States Court of Appeals, Ninth Circuit Aug 24, 1979 602 F.2d 1341 (9th Cir. 1979).
https://casetext.com/case/starker-v-united-states

41. **Family Limited Partnership:** Transferring limited partnership interests to family members reduces the taxable estate of senior family members. The senior family members transfer the value of the asset to their children, removing it from their estates for federal estate tax purposes, while retaining control over the decisions and distributions of the investment. Since the limited partners cannot control investments or distributions, they may be eligible for valuation discounts at the time of transfer. https://www.legalzoom.com/articles/flp-what-is-a-family-limited-partnership-and -how-can-it-save-your-family-money

42. **Limited Partners (LP):** Is a form of partnership similar to a general partnership except that while a general partnership must have at least two general partners (GPs), a limited partnership must have at least one GP and at least one limited partner. The GPs are, in all major respects, in the same legal position as partners in a conventional firm: They have management control, share the right to use partnership property, share the profits of the firm in predefined proportions, and have joint and several liabilities for the debts of the partnership. https://en.wikipedia.org/wiki/Limited_partnership

43. **Exchange Traded Funds:** Is an investment fund traded on stock exchanges, much like stocks. An ETF holds assets such as stocks, commodities, or bonds and generally operates with an arbitrage mechanism designed to keep it trading close to its net asset value, although deviations can occasionally occur. Most ETFs track an index, such as a stock index or bond index. ETFs may be attractive as investments because of their low costs, tax efficiency, and stock-like features. ETF distributors only buy or sell ETFs directly from or to authorized participants, which are large broker-dealers with whom they have entered into agreements—and then, only in creation units, which are large blocks of tens of thousands of ETF shares, usually exchanged in-kind with baskets of the underlying securities. https://en.wikipedia.org/wiki/Exchange-traded_fund

44. **Net Unrealized Appreciation (NUA):** When you retire or leave the company, you have two choices:

    Distribute the stock from the plan under special tax rules.

    Rollover all funds in cash to an IRA (you can also distribute the stock under special tax rules and then roll over the remainder of the funds to an IRA).

    If the company stock in your retirement plan was purchased with employer contributions or with your pre-tax contributions, then it is eligible for net unrealized appreciation tax treatment. It takes some calculating to determine if this special tax treatment will be beneficial for you. To understand how it works, let's walk through an example. https://www.thebalance.com/when-does-using-net-unrealized-appreciation-make -sense-2388276

45. **Tax Cut And Jobs Act Of 2017:** On November 2, 2017, Chairman Kevin Brady (R-TX) of the House Committee on Ways and Means released a tax reform plan, known as the House Tax Cuts and Jobs Act. The plan would reform the individual income tax code by lowering tax rates on wages, investment, and business income; broadening the tax base; and simplifying the tax code. The plan would lower the corporate income tax rate to 20 percent and move the United States from a world-wide to a territorial system of taxation. Our analysis finds that the plan would reduce

marginal tax rates on labor and investment. As a result, we estimate that the plan would increase long-run GDP by 3.5 percent. The larger economy would translate into 2.7 percent higher wages and result in 890,000 more full-time equivalent jobs. https://taxfoundation.org/2017-tax-cuts-jobs-act-analysis/

46. **Qualified Charitable Distributions:** What is a qualified charitable distribution? Generally, a qualified charitable distribution is an otherwise taxable distribution from an IRA (other than an ongoing SEP or SIMPLE IRA) owned by an individual who is age 70 1/2 or over that is paid directly from the IRA to a qualified charity. See Publication 590-B, Distributions from Individual Retirement Arrangements (IRAs) for additional information.
https://www.irs.gov/retirement-plans/retirement-plans-faqs-regarding-iras
-distributions-withdrawals

47. **Topics—403(b) Contribution Limits:** Generally, contributions to an employee's 403(b) account are limited to the lesser of:
    The limit on annual additions, or
    The elective deferral limit
    Limit On Employee Elective Salary Deferrals: The limit on elective deferrals—the most an employee can contribute to a 403(b) account out of salary—is $19,500 in 2020 ($19,000 in 2019). Employees who are age 50 or over at the end of the calendar year can also make catch-up contributions of $6,500 in 2020 beyond the basic limit on elective deferrals.
    https://www.irs.gov/retirement-plans/plan-participant-employee/retirement-topics
    -403b-contribution-limits

48. **Roth 403(b):** A designated Roth account is a separate account in a 401(k), 403(b) or governmental 457(b) plan that holds designated Roth contributions. The amount contributed to a designated Roth account is includible in gross income in the year of the contribution, but eligible distributions from the account (including earnings) are generally tax free. The employer must separately account for all contributions, gains and losses to this designated Roth account until this account balance is completely distributed.
    https://www.irs.gov/retirement-plans/retirement-plans-faqs-on-designated-roth
    -accounts

49. **457 Plans:** Is a type of non-qualified, tax advantaged deferred-compensation retirement plan that is available for governmental and certain non-governmental employers in the United States. The employer provides the plan and the employee defers compensation into it on a pre-tax or after-tax (Roth) basis. For the most part the plan operates similarly to a 401(k) or 403(b) plan most people are familiar with in the US. The key difference is that unlike with a 401(k) plan, there is no 10% penalty for withdrawal before the age of 55 (59 for IRA accounts) (although the withdrawal is subject to ordinary income taxation). 457 plans (both governmental and non-governmental) can also allow independent contractors to participate in the plan where 401(k) and 403(b) plans cannot.
    https://en.wikipedia.org/wiki/457_plan

50. **457 Catch-Up:** The 457 plan allows for two types of catch-up provisions. The first is similar to other defined contribution plans and amounts to an additional $6,000

that can be contributed as noted above. This option for making catch-up contributions is only available under governmental 457 plans. The second option is much more complicated and is available under both governmental and non-governmental plans. It can be elected by an employee who is within 3 years of normal retirement age (and perhaps eligible retirement at any age). This second catch-up option is equal to the full employee deferral limit or another $18,000 for 2017. Thus, a person over 50 within 3 years of retirement and who has both a 457 and a 401(k) could defer a total of $62,000 [18,000 + 18,000 for 457 and 18,000 + 8,000 for 401(k)] into his retirement plans by utilizing all of his catch-up provisions. The second type of catch-up provision is limited to unused deferral limits from previous years. An employee who had deferred the maximum amount of money into the 457 plan every year he was employed previously would not be able to utilize this extra catch-up.
https://en.wikipedia.org/wiki/457_plan

51. **Elective Deferrals:** Are amounts contributed to a plan by the employer at the employee's election and which, except to the extent they are designated Roth contributions, are excludable from the employee's gross income. Elective deferrals include deferrals under a 401(k), 403(b), SARSEP and SIMPLE IRA plan.
https://www.irs.gov/retirement-plans/plan-participant-employee/definitions

52. **Catch-Up Contributions:** SIMPLE Plan Catch-Up Amounts—A SIMPLE IRA or a SIMPLE 401(k) plan may permit annual catch-up contributions up to $3,000 in 2015—2020. Salary reduction contributions in a SIMPLE IRA plan are not treated as catch-up contributions until they exceed $13,500 in 2020 ($13,000 in 2015—2019).
403(b) Plan Catch-Up Amounts: Employees with at least 15 years of service may be eligible to make additional contributions to a 403(b) plan in addition to the regular catch-up for participants who are age 50 or over. See the discussion of 403(b) Contribution Limits for details.
IRA Catch-Up Amounts: You can make catch-up contributions to your traditional or Roth IRA up to $1,000 in 2015—2020. Catch-up contributions to an IRA are due by the due date of your tax return (not including extensions).
https://www.irs.gov/retirement-plans/plan-participant-employee/retirement-topics-catch-up-contributions

53. **ROTH Contributions:** A Roth IRA can be an individual retirement account containing investments in securities, usually common stocks and bonds, often through mutual funds (although other investments, including derivatives, notes, certificates of deposit, and real estate are possible). A Roth IRA can also be an individual retirement annuity, which is an annuity contract or an endowment contract purchased from a life insurance company. As with all IRAs, the Internal Revenue Service mandates specific eligibility and filing status requirements. A Roth IRA's main advantages are its tax structure and the additional flexibility that this tax structure provides. Also, there are fewer restrictions on the investments that can be made in the plan than many other tax-advantaged plans, and this adds somewhat to their popularity, though the investment options available depend on the trustee (or the place where the plan is established). 2019 age 49 and below $6,000, Age 50 and above $7,000. The Roth IRA was established by the Taxpayer Relief Act of 1997.
https://en.wikipedia.org/wiki/Roth_IRA

54. **Retirement Topics—SIMPLE IRA Contribution Limits**
    Salary Reduction Contributions: The amount an employee contributes from their salary to a SIMPLE IRA cannot exceed $13,500 in 2020 ($13,000 in 2019 and $12,500 in 2015—2018).
    If an employee participates in any other employer plan during the year and has elective salary reductions under those plans, the total amount of the salary reduction contributions that an employee can make to all the plans he or she participates in is limited to $19,500 in 2020 ($19,000 in 2019). See more than one plan.
    Catch-up contributions. If permitted by the SIMPLE IRA plan, participants who are age 50 or over at the end of the calendar year can also make catch-up contributions. The catch-up contribution limit for SIMPLE IRA plans is $3,000 in 2015—2020.
    https://www.irs.gov/retirement-plans/plan-participant-employee/retirement-topics-simple-ira-contribution-limits

55. **IRS 590-A:** This publication discusses contributions to individual retirement arrangements (IRAs). An IRA is a personal savings plan that gives you tax advantages for setting aside money for retirement. For information about distributions from an IRA, see Publication 590-B, Distributions from Individual Retirement Arrangements (IRAs).
    https://www.irs.gov/forms-pubs/about-publication-590-a

56. **SECURE Act Of 2019:** The SECURE Act changed the most popular retirement plans used in the United States and was the first major retirement-related legislation enacted since the 2006 Pension Protection Act. Major elements of the bill include: raising the minimum age for required minimum distributions from 70.5 years of age to 72 years of age; allowing workers to contribute to traditional IRAs after turning 70.5 years of age; allowing individuals to use 529 plan money to repay student loans; eliminating the so-called stretch IRA by requiring non-spouse beneficiaries of inherited IRAs to withdraw and pay taxes on all distributions from inherited accounts within 10 years; and making it easier for 401(k) plan administrators to offer annuities.
    https://en.wikipedia.org/wiki/SECURE_Act_of_2019

57. **Albert Einstein:** "Compound interest is the eighth wonder of the world. He who understands it, earns it . . . he who doesn't . . . pays it."
    https://www.goodreads.com/quotes/76863-compound-interest-is-the-eighth-wonder-of-the-world-he

58. **Delaware Senator William Victor Roth Jr.:** July 22, 1921—December 13, 2003, was an American lawyer and politician from Wilmington, Delaware. He was a veteran of World War II and a member of the Republican Party. He served from 1967 to 1970 as the lone U.S. Representative from Delaware and from 1971 to 2001 as a U.S. Senator from Delaware. Roth was a sponsor of legislation creating the Roth IRA, an individual retirement plan that can be set up with a broker.
    https://en.wikipedia.org/wiki/William_Roth

59. **Windfall Elimination Provision (WEP):** Can affect how we calculate your retirement or disability benefit. If you work for an employer who doesn't withhold Social Security taxes from your salary, such as a government agency or an employer in another country, any retirement or disability pension you get from that work can re-

duce your Social Security benefit. Before 1983, people whose primary job wasn't covered by Social Security had their Social Security benefits calculated as if they were long-term, low-wage workers. They had the advantage of receiving a Social Security benefit representing a higher percentage of their earnings, plus a pension from a job for which they didn't pay Social Security taxes. Congress passed the Windfall Elimination Provision to remove that advantage. Under the provision, they reduced the 90 percent factor in the formula and phased it in for workers who reached age 62 or became disabled between 1986 and 1989. For people who reach 62 or became disabled in 1990 or later, they reduced the 90 percent factor to as little as 40 percent. https://www.ssa.gov/pubs/EN-05-10045.pdf

60. **The Government Pension Offset (GPO):** A law that affects spouses and widows or widowers. If you receive a retirement or disability pension from a federal, state, or local government based on your own work for which you didn't pay Social Security taxes, we may reduce your Social Security spouses or widows or widowers benefits. This fact sheet provides answers to questions you may have about the reduction. https://www.ssa.gov/pubs/EN-05-10007.pdf

61. **Personal Earnings And Benefit Estimate Statement (PEBES):** Congress mandated that the Social Security Administration (SSA) send all workers an annual Personal Earnings and Benefit Estimate Statement (PEBES) by fiscal year 2000. SSA has been phasing in the mailing since April 1995. By the end of this calendar year, all workers aged 47and older should receive a PEBES. Beginning in October 1999, the mailings will become an annual process and will expand to include all workers age 25 and older. It is important to note, however, that the statements are not adjusted for the Windfall Elimination Provision or the Government Pension Offset, which may mislead some employees about future benefits. https://www.opm.gov/retirement-services/publications-forms/benefits-administration -letters/1998/98-110.pdf

62. **Single Life Annuity (SLA):** An annuity that only provides payments to one person. That is, payments cease when the annuitant dies. This contrasts with other annuities that make a lump sum payment to the annuitant's survivors, or continue payments to them for a certain number of years. Financial-dictionary.thefreedictionary.com/Single+life+annuity

63. **Joint And Survivor Pension Annuity:** Is an insurance product that continues regular payments as long as one annuitant is alive. A joint and survivor annuity must have two or more annuitants and married couples often purchase them to guarantee a surviving spouse receives a regular income for life. www.investopedia.com/terms/j/jointandsurvivorannuity.asp

64. **Life Annuity Certain And Continuous:** Is a type of annuity that guarantees a number of payments, even if the annuitant dies. If the annuitant passes away during the guaranteed period, a specified beneficiary will receive the rest of the payments. https://www.investopedia.com/terms/c/certain-and-continuous.asp

65. **North American Company For Health And Life Insurance:** This company is rated A+ by A.M. Best. It offers level premium policies that are convertible to permanent life insurance through age 74. This is a good option if you think a term policy will

work for you but might need a permanent policy, instead. The company offers a wide variety of riders, including one that waives certain monthly expenses if you become permanently disabled. Another rider allows you to extend the death benefit beyond the initial term, up to age 120.
https://www.northamericancompany.com/explore-life-insurance

66. **3307.563 Interest Added To Withdrawn Contributions:** For the purposes of this section, "service credit" includes only service credit obtained pursuant to sections 3307.53, 3307.71, 3307.712, 3307.72, and 3307.77 of the Revised Code.
http://codes.ohio.gov/orc/3307.563

67. **Revocable Living Trust:** A revocable living trust is a popular estate planning tool that you can use to determine who will get your property when you die. Most living trusts are "revocable" because you can change them as your circumstances or wishes change. Revocable living trusts are "living" because you make them during your lifetime.
https://www.nolo.com/legal-encyclopedia/revocable-living-trusts.html
(Also See)
Living Trust: Sometimes simply called a living trust—is a legal entity created to hold ownership of an individual's assets. The person who forms the trust is called the grantor or trust maker, and in most cases, also serves as the trustee, controlling and managing the assets placed there. Some trust makers prefer to have an institution or attorney acts as trustee, although this is somewhat uncommon with this type of trust. A revocable living trust covers three phases of the trust maker's life: his lifetime, possible incapacitation, and what happens after his death.
https://www.thebalance.com/what-is-a-revocable-living-trust-3505191

68. **Chapter 2113: EXECUTORS AND ADMINISTRATORS—APPOINTMENT; POWERS; DUTIES 2113.01:** What court shall grant letters. Upon the death of a resident of this state who dies intestate, letters of administration of the decedent's estate shall be granted by the probate court of the county in which the decedent was a resident at the time of death. If the will of any person is admitted to probate in this state, letters testamentary or of administration shall be granted by the probate court in which the will was admitted to probate.
http://codes.ohio.gov/orc/2113

69. **Ohio PERS Offers The Partial Lump Sum Option Payment (PLOP):** Is an option at retirement that allows a recipient to initially receive a lump sum benefit payment along with a reduced monthly retirement allowance.
https://www.opers.org/pubs-archive/PLOP%20Oct2009.pdf

70. **OPERS Pension And Healthcare Eligibility Guide Online:** As an OPERS member, your retirement security is our mission. But it's not always clear when members qualify both for their pension benefit and access to healthcare coverage through OPERS. This guide will help.
https://www.opers.org/members/pension-hc-eligibility/

71. **State Teachers Retirement System (STRS):** Is one of the nation's premier retirement systems, serving nearly 494,000 active, inactive and retired Ohio public educators. With investment assets of $79.9 billion (including short-term investments)

as of June 30, 2018, STRS Ohio is one of the largest public pension funds in the country. Learn more about STRS Ohio's impact in supporting and sustaining the state of Ohio.

https://www.strsoh.org/aboutus/strs-ohio/mission.html

72. **Alternative Retirement Plan (ARP):** All full-time faculty and staff members who are appointed to work at least 75 percent full-time equivalencies (FTE) are eligible to enroll in the Alternative Retirement Plan (ARP).

http://www.wright.edu/human-resources/benefits/retirement/state-teachers
-retirement-system-strs

73. **Ohio Defined Benefit Plan:** The Defined Benefit Plan is a plan that provides benefits during an STRS Ohio member's career and in retirement.

Under the Defined Benefit Plan, retirement income is determined by a calculation that uses a member's:

Age,

Years of service, and

Final average salary (FAS) — the average of their five highest salary years.

Members' benefits are created by three sources:

Their contributions during their career — they currently contribute 14% of their annual salary.

Their employer's contributions during their career.

Investment earnings resulting from those contributions.

Contribution rates are established by the State Teachers Retirement Board and are subject to change.

STRS Ohio maintains a diversified portfolio strategically allocated among stocks and fixed income, real estate, international and alternative investments. STRS Ohio investment professionals manage these funds so that benefits are there for members at retirement.

https://www.strsoh.org/aboutus/impact/db.html

74. **STRS Speech By Bob Buerkle To STRS Board:** "You need to unravel this mess" dated 02/21/2019. He went on to say, "Bureaucracy is a construction by which you are conveniently separated from the consequences of your actions." At STRS the Management Bureaucracy has no skin in our pension game. Instead, they have skin in the OPERS pension Game!

https://kathiebracy.blogspot.com/2019/03/bob-buerkle-to-strs-board-you-need
-to.html

75. **Ohio's Police And Fire Board Of Trustees:** Ohio law provides for the board to be comprised of nine members as follows. Six employee members elected by their respective member groups—two representatives of police departments, two representatives of fire departments, one retired police officer, and one retired firefighter. Three statutory members with professional investment experience—one appointed by the governor, one appointed by the state treasurer, one appointed jointly by the senate president and the speaker of the house.

https://www.op-f.org/boardoftrustees

76. **Registered Investment Advisor (RIA):** Is a "person or firm that, for compensation, is engaged in the act of providing advice, making recommendations, issuing reports

or furnishing analyses on securities, either directly or through publications" according to The Investment Advisers Act of 1940.
https://www.thebalance.com/what-is-a-registered-investment-advisor-357220

77. **Consumer Price Index (CPI):** Is a measure of the average change over time in the prices paid by urban consumers for a market basket of consumer goods and services. Indexes are available for the U.S. and various geographic areas. Average price data for select utility, automotive fuel and food items are also available.
https://www.bls.gov/cpi/

78. **OP&F Also Has A Brochure About The Death Benefit Fund:** In 1976, the 111th General Assembly established the Ohio Public Safety Officers Death Benefit Fund to provide special benefits to eligible survivors of public safety officers who are killed in the line of duty or who die of injuries or diseases incurred in the performance of official duties. The benefit is administered by the Ohio Police & Fire Pension Fund (OP&F) and is financed through legislative appropriations and gifts.
https://www.op-f.org/Files/MGdeath_benefit.pdf

79. **Executive Director John Gallagher Of OP&F:** Is under fire for "Healthcare Insurance After Retirement." And restricting retirees in their healthcare reimbursements for premiums.
https://lawofficer.com/editorial/ohios-betrayal-the-update/

80. **Aon Retiree Health Exchange:** In the spring of 2017 the OP&F Board of Trustees made the decision to restructure the retiree healthcare plan, ending the group-sponsored model that was in place for several years. A new model is currently scheduled to be implemented on Jan. 1, 2019, and will provide eligible retirees with a fixed monthly stipend earmarked to pay for healthcare. OP&F, through its partner, Aon, will assist in finding the right plan for each retiree.
https://www.op-f.org/Members/2019RetireeHealthCareTransition.aspx

81. **eHealth:** Is one of a handful of private companies that operate in partnership with the various government-run health insurance exchanges created as part of the Patient Protection and Affordable Care Act legislation. eHealth has been politically active on issues related to health insurance. Advertises itself as America's first and largest private online marketplace for health insurance, with the company inception in 1997.
https://en.wikipedia.org/wiki/EHealthInsurance

82. **State Employee Retirement System (SERS):** Provides retirement security for Ohio's non-teaching school employees, including administrative assistants, bus drivers, food service workers, librarians, maintenance personnel, teacher aides, and treasurers. Of the 81,332 individuals receiving pension benefits from SERS, 91% live in Ohio.
https://www.ohsers.org/about-sers/by-the-numbers/sers-fast-facts/

83. **SERS Marketplace Wraparound Plan:** 2020 Member Healthcare Guide Introduction. This guide is for future retirees and benefit recipients of the School Employees Retirement System of Ohio (SERS) who may be eligible for SERS' healthcare coverage. It provides information about current healthcare coverage and addresses a range of topics. The information in this guide is only an overview of the healthcare plans that are available and does not provide a complete description of each plan's coverage. When you enroll in SERS' healthcare coverage, you will receive a summary

of benefits. Coverage can be waived at any time. You can reenroll only if you have a qualifying event. Please see page 4 for more information. To the extent that resources permit, SERS intends to continue offering access to healthcare coverage. However, SERS reserves the right to change or discontinue any plan or program at any time. If you have questions or need more details, email us at: healthcare@ohsers.org or call us toll-free at 800-878-5853. We are available Monday through Friday, 8 a.m. to 4:30 p.m. This information is effective January 1, 2020.
https://www. ohsers.org

84. **Highway Patrol Retirement System (HPRS):** Healthcare is not a statutory benefit and subject to change.
Administered and controlled solely by the discretion
of the retirement system boards
Must be financed solely by employer contributions
(Federal law) search-
prod.lis.state.oh.us/.../retirementstudycouncilpresentation.pdf
https://www.ohsers.org/wp-content/uploads/2018/09/Member-Health-Care-Guide.pdf

85. **Here's The Average Length Of Retirement:** The average length of retirement: 18 years. What is the average length of retirement? It was recently 18 years, according to data from the U.S. Census Bureau. Meanwhile, the average age at which people retire these days is 63. That gives a typical retiree a retirement that lasts from about age 63 to about age 81. (The age at which most people start collecting Social Security, meanwhile, is 62—the earliest age at which they can do so).
https://www.fool.com/retirement/2018/02/24/heres-the-average-length-of-retirement
-will-your-m.aspx

86. **Reality Check:** Here's what the average retiree spends every month By Dayana Yochim: According to the latest Bureau of Labor Statistics data, which is based on 2016 figures, "older households" — defined as those run by someone 65 and older — spend an average of $45,756 a year, or roughly $3,800 a month. That's about $1,000 less than the monthly average spent by all U.S. households combined. Naturally, your spending in retirement will vary based on countless variables, including the price of your preferred champagne and the annual property taxes on that lake house (if those things happen to be on your retirement vision board). Read on to learn how retirees' spending habits tend to differ from the working population, and how you can plan for your personal post-work needs.
https://www.marketwatch.com/story/reality-check-what-the-average-retiree-spends
-a-month-2018-06-05

87. **American Time Use Survey:** Measures the amount of time people spend doing various activities, such as paid work, childcare, volunteering, and socializing.
https://www.bls.gov/tus/

88. **Health Savings Account (HSA):** A type of savings account that lets you set aside money on a pre-tax basis to pay for qualified medical expenses. By using untaxed dollars in a Health Savings Account (HSA) to pay for deductibles, copayments, co-insurance, and some other expenses, you may be able to lower your overall healthcare

costs. HSA funds generally may not be used to pay premiums. While you can use the funds in an HSA at any time to pay for qualified medical expenses, you may contribute to an HSA only if you have a High Deductible Health Plan (HDHP) — generally a health plan (including a Marketplace plan) that only covers preventive services before the deductible. For plan year 2019, the minimum deductible is $1,350 for an individual and $2,700 for a family. For plan year 2020, the minimum deductible for an HDHP is $1,400 for an individual and $2,800 for a family. When you view plans in the Marketplace, you can see if they're "HSA-eligible." https://www.healthcare.gov/glossary/health-savings-account-hsa/

89. **Healthcare During The Gap Years:** Publication 535—Introductory Material, Business Expenses: This publication discusses common business expenses and explains what is and is not deductible. The general rules for deducting business expenses are discussed in the opening chapter. The chapters that follow cover specific expenses and list other publications and forms you may need. Note: Section references within this publication are to the Internal Revenue Code and regulation references are to the Income Tax Regulations under the Code. https://www.irs.gov/publications/p535#en_US_2018_publink1000208599

90. **Dalai Lama:** "Man. Because he sacrifices his health in order to make money. Then he sacrifices money to recuperate his health. And then he is so anxious about the future that he does not enjoy the present; the result being that he does not live in the present or the future; he lives as if he is never going to die, and then dies having never really lived." https://www.mindbodygreen.com/0-6159/10-Inspiring-Quotes-From-the-Dalai -Lama.html

91. **Bureau Of Labor Statistics:** Table 1300. Age of reference person, Annual expenditure means, shares, standard errors, and coefficients of variation, Consumer Expenditure Survey, 2016. https://www.bls.gov/cex/2018/combined/age.pdf

92. **U.S. Bureau Of Labor Statistics CONSUMER EXPENDITURES— Expenditure Surveys CE Tables 2018:** This page provides links to tables with expenditure and income data calculated by the Consumer Expenditure Surveys. Some tables provide population means (as opposed to means of those reporting), percent shares, and variance measures (Standard Error and Coefficient of Variation). Other tables present aggregate expenditures and income and related aggregate percent shares. The tables first provide the most recent data and the links to tables for selected historical time periods. The latest midyear tables were released on April 26, 2019. The latest annual tables were released on September 10, 2019. https://www.bls.gov/cex/tables.htm **Average Expenditure, Share, And Standard Error Tables**: Age of reference person. https://www.bls.gov/cex/2018/combined/age.pdf

93. **Certified Financial Planner (CFP):** The mission of Certified Financial Planner Board of Standards, Inc. is to benefit the public by granting the CFP® certification and upholding it as the recognized standard of excellence for competent and ethical personal financial planning. The new Code and Standards takes effect Oct. 1, 2019,

and includes a range of important changes, including expanding the scope of the fiduciary standard that requires CFP® professionals to act in the best interest of the client at all times when providing financial advice.
https://www.cfp.net/

94. **Chartered Financial Analyst (CFA):** The mission of CFA Institute is served by generating value for core investment management professionals and engaging with the core investment management industry to advance ethics, market integrity, and professional standards of practice, which collectively contributes value to society. Core investment management professionals are those individuals primarily involved in activities related to the investment decision-making process—generally portfolio managers, financial advisors, and research analysts on both the buy and sell side. Trust: We act with integrity, are ethical and authentic, and speak the truth in a timely, transparent manner.
https://www.cfainstitute.org/en/about/vision

95. **Darren Hardy:** Is an American author, keynote speaker, advisor, and former publisher of SUCCESS magazine. Hardy is a New York Times best-selling author, who wrote The Entrepreneur Roller Coaster, Living Your Best Year Ever and The Compound Effect. Hardy started his first business at age 18. He has been a central figure in the success media business for 25+ years. In 2007 he became publisher of SUCCESS magazine and Success Media. In December 2015, Hardy announced he was leaving SUCCESS magazine as publisher to pursue new opportunities.
https://en.wikipedia.org/wiki/Darren_Hardy

96. **Dan Sullivan—Strategic Coach:** Is founder and president of The Strategic Coach Inc. A visionary, an innovator, and a gifted conceptual thinker, Dan has over 35 years' experience as a highly regarded speaker, consultant, strategic planner, and coach to entrepreneurial individuals and groups. Dan's strong belief in and commitment to the power of the entrepreneur is evident in all areas of Strategic Coach® and its successful coaching program, which works to help entrepreneurs reach their full potential in both their business and personal lives.
https://resources.strategiccoach.com/

CHARTS

Chart A—Source—National Center For Health Statistics—*Health, United States 2016:* Health, United States, 2016 is the 40th report on the health status of the nation and is submitted by the Secretary of the Department of Health and Human Services to the President and the Congress of the United States in compliance with Section 308 of the Public Health Service Act. This report was compiled by the Centers for Disease Control and Prevention's (CDC) National Center for Health Statistics (NCHS).
https://www.cdc.gov/nchs/data/hus/2016/015.pdf
https://www.cdc.gov/nchs/hus/description.htm

Chart B—Source—Saving Early—Bankrate Interest Calculator: Consistent investing over a long period of time can be an effective strategy to accumulate wealth. Even small deposits to a savings account can add up over time. This compound interest calculator demonstrates how to put this savings strategy to work. This table demonstrates the importance of starting early. It assumes an annual investment of $6,000, assumes a steady 6 percent annual re-turn, starts from the ages of 25, 35, and 45, and assumes retirement at age 65.
https://www.bankrate.com/calculators/savings/compound-savings-calculator-tool.aspx

TABLES

Table A—Source—Standard & Poor's: History starts in 1860. In 1906, Luther Lee Blake founded the Standard Statistics Bureau, with the view to providing financial information on non-railroad companies. Instead of an annually published book, Standard Statistics would use 5-by-7-inch cards, allowing for more frequent updates. In 1941, Paul Talbot Babson purchased Poor's Publishing and merged it with Standard Statistics to become Standard & Poor's Corp. In 1966, the company was acquired by The McGraw-Hill Companies, extending McGraw-Hill into the field of financial information services. https://en.wikipedia.org/wiki/Standard_ percent26_Poor percent27s#Credit_ratings

Fitch Ratings Inc.: The firm was founded by John Knowles Fitch on December 24, 1914 in New York City as the Fitch Publishing Company. In 1989, the company was acquired by a group including Robert Van Kampen. In 1997, Fitch was acquired by FIMALAC and was merged with London-based IBCA Limited, a FIMALAC subsidiary. In 2000 Fitch acquired both Chicago-based Duff & Phelps Credit Rating Co. (April) and Thomson Financial Bank-Watch (December).
https://en.wikipedia.org/wiki/Fitch_Ratings

Moody's Investors Service: Often referred to as Moody's, is the bond credit rating business of Moody's Corporation, representing the company's traditional line of business and its historical name. Moody's Investors Service provides international financial research on bonds issued by commercial and government entities. Moody's, along with Standard & Poor's and Fitch Group, is considered one of the Big Three credit rating agencies.
https://en.wikipedia.org/wiki/Moody%27s_Investors_Service

Table B—Source—Ohio Police & Firemen Retiree Healthcare Plan Monthly Stipend Levels As Of May 22, 2018: In the spring of 2017 the OP&F Board of Trustees made the decision to restructure the retiree healthcare plan, ending the group-sponsored model that was in place for several years. A new model has been implemented as of Jan. 1, 2019. This model will provide eligible retirees with a fixed stipend earmarked to pay for healthcare. OP&F, through its partner, Aon, will assist in finding the right plan for each retiree. It is OP&F's goal that the move to a new healthcare option will extend available funding for healthcare to approximately 15 years. Current projections show that without changes, funding for retiree healthcare will be depleted in less than 10 years.
https://www.op-f.org/retiredmembers/healthcare

Table C—Source—Net Unrealized Appreciation (NUA): This is a hypothetical illustration to show how an NUA Strategy would work. It does not reflect the tax or investment value of any specific investment, nor does it include other applicable fees or taxes.

Table D—Source—Adapted From "IRA Contribution Limits," Fidelity Investments: Traditional IRA contribution limits and eligibility are based on your modified adjusted gross income (MAGI), depending on tax-filing status. Partial contributions are allowed for certain income ranges.
https://www.fidelity.com/retirement-ira/contribution-limits-deadlines

Table E—Source—Adapted From "IRA Contribution Limits," Fidelity Investments: Roth IRA contribution limits and eligibility are based on your modified adjusted gross income (MAGI), depending on tax-filing status. Partial contributions are allowed for certain income ranges.
https://www.fidelity.com/retirement-ira/contribution-limits-deadlines

Table F—Source—Adapted From "Traditional and Roth IRAs," Internal Revenue Service: Traditional and Roth IRAs allow you to save money for retirement. This chart highlights some of their similarities and differences.
https://www.irs.gov/retirement-plans/traditional-and-roth-iras

Table G—Source—Adapted From "Roth Comparison Chart," Internal Revenue Service: Roth 401(k), Roth IRA, and Pre-tax 401(k) Retirement Accounts.
https://www.irs.gov/retirement-plans/roth-comparison-chart

Table H—Source—Adapted From "Windfall Elimination Provision," Social Security Administration: Is a formula used to adjust Social Security worker benefits for people who receive "non-covered pensions" and qualify for Social Security benefits based on other Social Security-covered earnings. A non-covered pension is a pension paid by an employer that does not withhold Social Security taxes from your salary, typically, state and local governments or non-U.S. employers. Congress passed the WEP to prevent workers who receive non-covered pensions from receiving higher Social Security benefits as if they were long-time, low-wage earners. In 2013, the WEP applied to approximately 2.5 percent of all beneficiaries (1.5 million beneficiaries).
https://www.ssa.gov/pubs/EN-05-10045.pdf

Table I—Source—Adapted From "Windfall Elimination Provision" (WEP) Chart, Social Security Administration: The chart shows the maximum monthly amount your benefit can be reduced because of WEP if you have fewer than 30 years of substantial earnings. (To calculate your WEP reduction, please use our WEP Online Calculator or download our Detailed Calculator.)
https://www.ssa.gov/planners/retire/wep-chart.html

Table J—Source—Numbers Generated Via "Calculate Your Benefits," Government Pension Offset—Social Security Administration: If you receive a retirement or disability pension from a federal, state, or local government based on your own work for which you didn't pay Social Security taxes, we may reduce your Social Security spouses or widows or widowers benefits. This fact sheet provides answers to questions you may have about the reduction.
https://www.ssa.gov/pubs/EN-05-10007.pdf

Table K—Source—Adapted From "Account Withdrawal," STRS Ohio: Upon termination of public employment in Ohio, you may elect to withdraw your account. It is important to understand that withdrawing your STRS Ohio account is not a type of service retirement. Withdrawal of your account will cancel your STRS Ohio membership,

your accumulated service credit and your eligibility to qualify for STRS Ohio retirement benefits, including access to healthcare coverage, if eligible.
https://www.strsoh.org/actives/teaching/withdrawal.html

Table L—Source—Adapted From "Benefit Recipient Handbook," OPERS: Retirement Plans, Retirement benefits are based on contributions to one or more of the following retirement plans: The Traditional Pension Plan is a defined benefit plan under which a member's retirement benefit is calculated on a formula based on years of service, final average salary, and a percentage. Members who retire through the Traditional Pension Plan receive a monthly age and service benefit. The Member-Directed Plan is a defined contribution plan under which employee and a portion of the employer contributions are deposited into a member's individual defined contribution account and invested as directed by the member. The Combined Plan is made up of two components. OPERS manage employer contributions used to fund the defined benefit portion at retirement. The retirement benefit for the defined benefit component is determined by a formula based on years of service, final average salary, and a percentage. The member chooses the investment options for employee contributions in the defined contribution portion. The retirement benefit for this portion is based on the employee contributions and the gains and losses on those contributions.
https://www.opers.org/pubs-archive/retirees/Benefit-Recipient-Handbook.pdf

Table M—Source—Adapted From Ohio Public Employees Retirement System, For Qualified Non-Medicare Participants: The OPERS healthcare program provides access to group coverage or access to funding that provides reimbursement for qualified healthcare expenses. The type of pension plan, Traditional, Combined or Member-Directed, you chose early in your public career and your Medicare status will determine what healthcare program options you have available. The following explains these options.
https://www.opers.org/pubs-archive/healthcare/open/2016/OE%20FAQ.pdf.
https://www.opers.org/pubs-archive/healthcare/coverage-guide/coverage-guide-2019.pdf

Table N—Source—Adapted From "DROP (Deferred Retirement Option Plan) Information," Ohio Police And Fire Pension Fund: Subject to change. Please check for updated posted rates from the OP&F before making any decisions. At its October meeting, the OP&F Board of Trustees approved a change in the Deferred Retirement Option Plan (DROP) interest rate that will benefit participants in the program. Beginning Jan. 1, 2020, a 2.5 percent minimum interest rate will accrue for OP&F members participating in DROP. A maximum rate of 5.0 percent remains in place. Interest credited to DROP balances each month will continue to be calculated at a rate equal to the 10-year U.S. Treasury Note Business Day Series, as published by the United States Federal Reserve (updated quarterly). However, once the change is implemented, DROP participants will receive a rate between 2.5 and 5.0 on their DROP accrual while it is at OP&F. The change was made in recognition of the current low interest rate environment in the U.S. financial system. The rate has dipped as low as 1.49 percent, and was set at 1.68 percent for the fourth quarter of 2019. The minimum rate will provide more stability and predictability for the DROP accruals members have deposited at OP&F.
https://www.op-f.org/information/opfnewshigher-drop-interest-rate-approved-by-board/7397

Table O—Source—OHIO Police & Fire: Sample Single Life versus 50% Joint & Survivor Pension Payout. Complete a thorough analysis of joint survivor payout options. One

of the common mistakes made in the calculation of survivor payout options is that most people believe there are only two pension payout options: life only and joint survivor. In fact, there are several survivorship options to choose from, including 100%, 75%, 50% and many more. If you want to make allowances for your spouse, for example a 50% joint survivor option will reduce your pension payout about 10% (depending on age and length of service) to provide benefits during his or her lifetime. If you are to receive $60,000 per annum in life only, you'll receive approximately $54,000 in order to provide your spouse $27,000 per annum during his/her lifetime. DON'T FORGET, Cost of Living Adjustments (COLA) are based on your pension payout so if you choose to take the life only option you will dramatically increase your pension payouts in the future. The additional $6,000 per year, compounded at 3% over your lifetime can add up to hundreds of thousands of additional dollars in income during retirement.
https://ohioretire.com/eliminate-spousal-pension-shortfalls-under-opf

Table P—Source—OP&F Retiree Healthcare Plan (Updated August 8th, 2018): The latest information concerning retiree healthcare benefits is featured below. Additional information from our healthcare partner, Aon Retiree Health Exchange, can be found at a special website for OP&F members. In the spring of 2017, the OP&F Board of Trustees made the decision to restructure the retiree healthcare plan, ending the group-sponsored model that was in place for several years. A new model has been implemented as of Jan. 1, 2019. This model will provide eligible retirees with a fixed stipend earmarked to pay for healthcare. OP&F, through its partner, Aon, will assist in finding the right plan for each retiree. It is OP&F's goal that the move to a new healthcare option will extend available funding for healthcare to approximately 15 years. Current projections show that without changes, funding for retiree healthcare will be depleted in less than 10 years. To learn more, go to: retiree.aon.com/op-f
https://www.op-f.org/retiredmembers/healthcare

Table Q—Source—Adapted From "Service Credit," School Employees Retirement System Of Ohio: Service credit is accrued through contributions during school employment and for other service that may be purchased.
The amount of your service credit determines:
- Your eligibility for retirement or disability benefits
- The amount of your payment
- Your eligibility for healthcare coverage and the amount of your premium

It also determines the eligibility of your dependents for survivor benefits, the amount of benefits, and availability of healthcare coverage.
https://www.ohsers.org/members/working-members/service-credit/

Table R—Source—Adapted From "HPRS Investment Returns," Highway Patrol Retirement System: 2017 was an outstanding year for investment returns for HPRS, earning approximately 14.4% over the course of the year. These results increased the value of the pension fund to over $900 million from approximately $825 million at the end of 2016. This increase in value is particularly encouraging when you consider that HPRS paid out $70 million in pension benefits and $15 million in healthcare benefits during 2017. And while these are excellent results, we cannot lose sight of our long-term goal. HPRS must not only be able to provide benefits for current retirees, but must also remain solvent for those troopers entering the system today who will not retire for 25-30 years.
https://www.ohprs.org/ohprs/downloads/newsletters/March%202018.pdf

WORKS CITED

Books

Hardy, Darren. *The Compound Effect: Jumpstart Your Income, Your Life, Your Success.* New York: Vanguard Press, 2011.

Journals

U Techera, M Hallowell, N Stambaugh, R. Littlejohn, "Causes and consequences of occupational fatigue: meta-analysis and systems model," *Journal of Occupational and Environmental Medicine:* 58 no 10 (October 2018): 961–973. Accessed online. (https://journals.lww.com/joem/Abstract/2016/10000/Causes_and_Consequences_of_Occupational_Fatigue__.1.aspx)

Pamphlets/Brochures

Highway Patrol Retirement System, *Quarterly Newsletter,* March 2018, https://www.ohprs.org/ohprs/downloads/newsletters/March%202018.pdf

Ohio Police & Fire Pension Fund, *Member's Guide to: Disability Benefits,* updated May 2018. https://www.op-f.org/Files/MGDisabilityBenefits.pdf

Ohio Police & Fire Pension Fund, *Member's Guide to Survivor Benefits,* https://www.opf.org/(S(lvpnet41ln5x0xtumffefvv0))/Files/Members_Guide_to_Survivor_Benefits.pdf

Ohio Public Employees Retirement System, *2019 Healthcare Coverage Guide,* revised November 2018. https://www.opers.org/pubs-archive/healthcare/coverage-guide/coverage-guide-2019.pdf

Ohio Public Employees Retirement System, "Benefit Recipient Handbook," revised August 2013.

Ohio Public Employees Retirement System, *Pension and Healthcare Eligibility Guide,* March 2019. https://www.opers.org/pubs-archive/members/2019-03-PNSHCELIGGUIDE-Pension -and-Health-Care-Eligibility-Guide.pdf

Social Security Administration, *Government Pension Offset*, February 2017.
https://www.ssa.gov/pubs/EN-05-10007.pdf

Social Security Administration, *Windfall Elimination Provision*, 2019.
https://www.ssa.gov/pubs/EN-05-10045.pdf

U.S. Department of Health and Human Services, *Health, United States, 2016, with Chartbook on Long-term Trends in Health.*
https://www.cdc.gov/nchs/data/hus/hus16.pdf#015

Ohio Stare Pension Fund Websites

Ohio Highway Patrol Retirement System, updated 2019.
https://www.ohprs.org/ohprs/

Ohio Police & Fire Pension Fund, updated 2019.
https://www.op-f.org/

Ohio Public Employees Retirement System, updated 2019.
https://www.opers.org/

School Employees Retirement System of Ohio, updated 2019.
https://www.ohsers.org/

State Teachers Retirement System of Ohio, updated 2019.
https://www.strsoh.org/

Websites

"2019 Retiree Healthcare Transition," OP&F.
https://www.opf.org/Members/2019RetireeHealthCareTransition.aspx

"3307.563 Interest added to withdrawn contributions," LAWriter: Ohio Laws and Rules, updated October 1, 2002.
http://codes.ohio.gov/orc/3307.563

"About Publication 590-A, Contributions to Individual Retirement Arrangements (IRAs)," Internal Revenue Service, updated April 2, 2019.
https://www.irs.gov/forms-pubs/about-publication-590-a

"About Publication 590-B, Distributions from Individual Retirement Arrangements (IRAs)," IRS, updated September 25, 2018.
https://www.irs.gov/forms-pubs/about-publication-590-b

"About Us," Iron Workers Local Union No. 17.
https://www.iw17.org/about/

Abramowicz, Lisa, "5% Is the New 8% for Pension Funds," Bloomberg Businessweek, August 2, 2017.
https://www.bloomberg.com/news/articles/2017-08-02/5-is-the-new-8-for-reliable
-returns-for-pension-funds

"Account Withdrawal," STRS Ohio.
https://www.strsoh.org/actives/teaching/withdrawal.html

American Time Use Survey, Bureau of Labor Statistics.
https://www.bls.gov/tus/

Bischoff, Laura A., "Big returns help bolster Ohio's five public pension funds," *Dayton Daily News*, February 27, 2018.
https://www.daytondailynews.com/news/big-returns-help-bolster-ohio-five-public-pension-funds/61mj6w35nXeMflJhZrgvJP/

"Changing Your Plan of Payment: Joint & Survivor Annuity with Reversion," STRS.
https://www.strsoh.org/retirees/payments/payment-plan.html

"Combined Plan: Features of the Combined Plan," Ohio Public Employees Retirement System.
https://www.opers.org/members/combined/features.shtml

"Consumer Expenditure Surveys," Bureau of Labor Statistics.
https://www.bls.gov/cex/

"DROP (Deferred Retirement Option Plan) Information," Ohio Police & Fire Pension Fund.
https://www.op-f.org/Members/DropInformation.aspx

Elder, Erick M., and David Mitchell, "Ohio Public Pension System: Traditional Funding Ratios are not Enough for Pension Fund," Mercatus Center, George Mason University, December 2016.
https://www.mercatus.org/system/files/mercatus-elder-ohio-public-pension-v2.pdf

"Federal Reductions to Social Security Benefits of State and Local Employees: The Windfall Elimination Reduction and the Government Pension Offset," National Conference of State Legislatures, revised June 2000.
http://www.lobby.la.psu.edu/028_WEP_GPO/Organizational_Statements/NCSL/NCSL_Federal_Reducations_to_Social_Security_0600.htm

Financial Advisors with CFA designation (untitled post), Parabolic Asset Management, July 22, 2015.
https://parabolic.us/2015/07/what-percentage-of-financial-advisors/

"Financial State of the States," Truth in Accounting, September 19, 2017.
https://www.truthinaccounting.org/news/detail/financial-state-of-the-states-2-2

"Five Year End Strategies For the High Income Earner," Lineweaver Financial Group, (Passage reprinted with permission.)
https://www.lineweaver.net/five-year-end-strategies-for-te-high-income-earner.

"Forms and Publications," School Employees Retirement System of Ohio.
https://www.ohsers.org/members/forms-and-publications/

"Growing Your Wealth Through Real Estate," Lineweaver Financial Group. (Passage reprinted with permission.)
https://www.lineweaver.net/growing-your-wealth-through-real-estate

"Health Savings Account," Health Insurance.org.
https://www.healthinsurance.org/glossary/health-savings-account/

"Health Savings Accounts (HSAs)," U.S. Department of the Treasury.
https://www.treasury.gov/resource-center/faqs/Taxes/Pages/Health-Savings-Accounts
.aspx

"How Big Is Your State's Share of $6 Trillion in Unfunded Pension Liabilities?," The
Heritage Foundation, December 21, 2017.
https://www.heritage.org/budget-and-spending/commentary/how-big-your-states-share
-6-trillion-unfunded-pension-liabilities

"How Much Sleep Do We Really Need?" National Sleep Foundation,
https://www.sleepfoundation.org/excessive-sleepiness/support/how-much-sleep-do
-we-really-need

"How to plan for rising healthcare costs," Fidelity Investments, April 1, 2019.
https://www.fidelity.com/viewpoints/personal-finance/plan-for-rising-health-care
-costs

"H.R.1—An Act to provide for reconciliation pursuant to titles II and V of the concurrent
resolution on the budget for fiscal year 2018," Congress.gov.
https://www.congress.gov/bill/115th-congress/house-bill/1/text

"In unprecedented move, pension plan cuts benefits promised to retirees," Jonnelle Marte,
Washington Post, January 27, 2017.
https://www.washingtonpost.com/news/get-there/wp/2017/01/27/in-unprecedented
-move-pension-plan-approves-benefit-cuts-for-retired-iron-workers/?noredirect=on
&utm_term=.f21e85b6941b

"Investments," Ohio Deferred Compensation.
https://www.ohio457.org/iApp/tcm/ohio457/investments/index.jsp

"IRA Contribution Limits," Fidelity Investments.
https://www.fidelity.com/retirement-ira/contribution-limits-deadlines

"Iron Workers pension cuts approved; retirees to get smaller checks," Cleveland.com,
January 27, 2017.
https://www.cleveland.com/nation/2017/01/iron_workers_pension_cuts_are.html

"IRS Announces 2018 Pension Plan Limitations; 401(k) Contribution Limit Increases to
$18,500 for 2018," Internal Revenue Service, October 19, 2017.
https://www.irs.gov/newsroom/irs-announces-2018-pension-plan-limitations-401k
-contribution-limit-increases-to-18500-for-2018

"John M. Richardson (professor)," Infogalactic, updated November 2, 2015.
https://infogalactic.com/info/John_M._Richardson_(professor)

"Like-Kind Exchanges Under IRC Code Section 2031," IRS, February 2008.
https://www.irs.gov/newsroom/like-kind-exchanges-under-irc-code-section-1031

"List of U.S. states and territories by life expectancy," Wikipedia. Ohio ranks 39th of the
50 states with an average life expectancy of 77.8 years.
https://en.wikipedia.org/wiki/List_of_U.S._states_and_territories_by_life_expectancy

"Monthly Stipend Levels as of May 22, 2018," Ohio Police & Fire Pension Fund.
https://www.opf.org/Members/2019RetireeHealthCareTransition.aspx

More Support, More Choices with Aon Retiree Health Exchange (untitled post).
https://www.myexchangeconnection.com/OP-F/home#LearnTab

Norcross, Eileen, "Ranking the States' Fiscal Solvency," Public Sector Inc., January 14, 2014.
http://www.publicsectorinc.org/2014/01/ranking-the-states-fiscal-solvency/

"Number of Active CFP Professionals Reaches All-Time High," Think Advisor, September 6, 2016.
https://www.thinkadvisor.com/2016/09/06/number-of-active-cfp-professionals-reaches-all-tim/?slreturn=20190306220343

"Ohio lawmakers give final OK to public pension reforms," Cleveland.com, September 12, 2012.
https://www.cleveland.com/open/2012/09/ohio_lawmakers_give_final_ok_t.html

"Ohio Public Pension System," Mercatus Center at George Mason University, December 13, 2016.
www.mercatus.org/ohiopensions

"Ohio teachers want cost of living allowance restored," 10 WBNS, June 21, 2018.
https://www.10tv.com/article/ohio-teachers-want-cost-living-allowance-restored

"OP&F will move toward healthcare stipend in 2019," Ohio Police & Fire Pension Fund.
https://www.op-f.org/Information/ViewNews.aspx?Id=5903

"OPERS announces 2019 cost-of-living adjustment," Ohio Public Employees Retirement System PERSpective, July 24, 2018.
https://perspective.opers.org/index.php/2018/07/24/opers-announces-2019-cost-of-living-adjustment/

"OPERS Healthcare," Ohio Public Employees Retirement System.
https://www.opers.org/healthcare/

"Personal Financial Advisors," Bureau of Labor Statistics.
https://www.bls.gov/ooh/business-and-financial/personal-financial-advisors.htm

"Purchasing Service Credit Calculator," STRS Ohio.
https://www.strsoh.org/v10prdcalc/app?service=external/Client:NonSecurePSC100LBCalculator

Rauh, Joshua D., "Hidden Debt, Hidden Deficit: 2017 Edition: How Pension Promises Are Consuming State and Local Budgets," Hoover Institution, May 15, 2017.
https://www.hoover.org/research/hidden-debt-hidden-deficits-2017-edition

"Rawlings, Griggs Square Off Over Proposed Fixes to Dallas Police Pension," *Dallas Observer*, April 21, 2017.
http://www.dallasobserver.com/news/dallas-mayor-mike-rawlings-hates-police-pension-fix-9391589

"Retirement System Facts," School Employees Retirement System of Ohio.
https://www.ohsers.org/about-sers/by-the-numbers/sers-fast-facts/

"Roth Comparison Chart," Internal Revenue Service, updated November 8, 2018.
https://www.irs.gov/retirement-plans/roth-comparison-chart

"Sears Holdings Enters Into Arrangement To Pension Plan Protection Arrangement With PBGC," Sears Holdings, November 8, 2017.
https://searsholdings.com/press-releases/pr/2064

"Selecting a Plan of Payment," STRS Ohio.
https://www.strsoh.org/actives/retire-prep/payment-plan.html

"Service Credit," School Employees Retirement System of Ohio.
https://www.ohsers.org/members/working-members/service-credit/

Strategic Coach, Dan Sullivan.
https://www.strategiccoach.com/

"Summary of Retirement Benefits," Ohio Highway Patrol Retirement System.
https://www.ohprs.org/ohprs/retirementBenefits.jsp

"Taxpayer Relief Act of 1997," Congress.gov.
https://www.congress.gov/105/plaws/publ34/PLAW-105publ34.pdf

"The Best Explanation of the Windfall Elimination Provision," Social Security Intelligence.
https://socialsecurityintelligence.com/the-windfall-elimination-provision/

"The Time Bomb Inside Public Pension Plans," Wharton University of Pennsylvania, August 23, 2018.
https://knowledge.wharton.upenn.edu/article/the-time-bomb-inside-public-pension-plans/

"Traditional and Roth IRAs," Internal Revenue Service, updated November 6, 2018.
https://www.irs.gov/retirement-plans/traditional-and-roth-iras

Truth in Accounting, 2019.
https://www.truthinaccounting.org/

"US government pension shortfall overshadowed by Social Security, Medicare gaps," Moody's, April 6, 2016.
https://www.moodys.com/research/Moodys-US-government-pension-shortfall-overshadowed-by-Social-Security-Medicare--PR_346878

"U.S. Retirement Assets Reach $26 Trillion," American Society of Pension Professionals and Actuaries, June 28, 2017.
https://www.asppa.org/News/Article/ArticleID/8792

"What is a 1031 Exchange?," Asset Preservation Incorporated.
https://apiexchange.com/what-is-a-1031-exchange/

"What is Government Pension Offset (GPO)?," Social Security Administration.
https://www.ssa.gov/planners/retire/gpo-calc.html

"When to Start Your Benefits," Social Security Administration.
https://www.ssa.gov/planners/retire/applying1.html

"Will This Year's College Grads Job-Hop More Than Previous Grads?" LinkedIn Official Blog, April 12, 2016.
https://blog.linkedin.com/2016/04/12/will-this-year_s-college-grads-job-hop-more-than-previous-grads

"Windfall Elimination Provision (WEP) Chart," Social Security Administration.
https://www.ssa.gov/planners/retire/wep-chart.html

Young, Stephen, "Hidden Debt, Hidden Deficit: 2017 Edition: How Pension Promises Are Consuming State and Local Budgets," Hoover Institution, May 15, 2017.
https://www.hoover.org/research/hidden-debt-hidden-deficits-2017-edition

INDEX